Studies in Religious Experience

THIS TIME-BOUND LADDER

THIS TIME-BOUND LADDER

TEN DIALOGUES ON RELIGIOUS EXPERIENCE

Peter Baelz Rosalind Heywood
Carmen Blacker Martin Israel
Christopher Bryant Raynor Johnson
Monica Furlong Kallistos Ware
Lev Gillet Michael Whiteman
Freda Wint

Edited by
Edward Robinson

THE RELIGIOUS EXPERIENCE RESEARCH UNIT
MANCHESTER COLLEGE
OXFORD

ISBN 0 906165 02 4

We are grateful to Messrs. Faber and Faber for permission to quote from Louis MacNeice's *Springboard* (1944) the four lines of his poem *Prayer in Mid-passage* printed here on page 1.

We are grateful to the Hibbert Trust for their support and encouragement, and in particular for a generous grant towards the costs of publication.

Yet grant to men that they may climb
This time-bound ladder out of time
And by our human organs we
Shall thus transcend humanity.

Louis MacNeice

CONTENTS

Introduction

"I dislike the words 'religious experience'. I think they are the cause of great confusion, and I blame William James for having introduced such an idea." So says one of the participants in these dialogues. James should not perhaps be given the sole blame, or credit, for having invented the phrase, but it was certainly he who first gave currency, as well as substance, to the concept, and it is one that has become of steadily increasing interest in the seventy-five years since the publication of his famous Gifford Lectures. In fact *The Varieties of Religious Experience* nowhere gives us an explicit definition. He comes nearest to it in his "Circumscription of the Topic", with his well-known declaration that "religion . . . shall mean for us the feelings, acts, and experiences of individual men in their solitude, so far as they apprehend themselves to stand in relation to whatever they may consider the divine". Even this statement, however, he admits to be arbitrary; and not without its difficulties: what, for example, do we mean by "the divine"? So, perhaps not surprisingly, he arrives a few pages later at the position: "Religion, whatever it is, is a man's total reaction upon life" — though he adds that such a response must be solemn and grave. In much the same way Socrates, faced with the apparently simple problem of defining "courage" or "piety", would find himself having first to decide the whole question of the nature of good and evil. James is likewise caught up in the Socratic spiral, whose ever widening circles involve an examination of the whole of life before judgement can be passed on any single aspect of it.

It is very much in this Socratic spirit that I offer these ten dialogues. Religious experience is in fact a topic that is virtually impossible to circumscribe. The question mark on which the book ends seems to me entirely appropriate to conclude what is in fact a by-product of work in progress; and if you ask, "Progress towards what?" I can only hope that these discussions will themselves give some hint of what we are after, even if by the end the reader does not feel much nearer to a solution.

Solutions, however, as Marcel and other existentialist writers have pointed out, belong to the world of problems. Mysteries are of a different order altogether. It may be that science properly belongs only to the realm of the problematic, and should not aspire to be more than, in Sir Peter Medawar's phrase, "the art of the soluble". Philosophers, too, have tried to limit their liabilities. "Metaphysics", said Bradley, "is the finding of bad reasons for what we believe upon instinct." And since then other philosophers, in the name of empiricism, have been increasingly fastidious over the kind of experience they will allow to have any claim on their attention, like hypochondriacs who cannot face any but the most undemanding diet. But the presuppositions of anyone, whether scientist or philosopher, who attempts to give a systematic and consistent account of human experience are themselves a much more mysterious business. As Bradley went on to say, "To find these reasons is no less an instinct".

An instinct? It is man's self-consciousness that distinguishes him from all other animals, and this enables him to diverge from the instinctual pattern by which their lives are ruled. Man alone can reflect in universal terms that transcend the here and now, and so can come to conceive of, and indeed experience, a reality that lies beyond space and time. It was the neglect of this aspect of human consciousness in most previous studies of evolution that led Sir Alister Hardy to initiate this research project, and to issue the appeal that has brought in the remarkable body of accounts of personal experience which has formed the starting-point for our work. It is, however, an aspect that is peculiarly difficult to make the subject of a precise and systematic study. This is partly because, as I have said, this awareness of universality pervades the whole of man's thinking, though generally of course at a subliminal level. But the chief difficulty lies deeper than this.

The problem is, in the first place, one of language. We have words for concrete objects, we have words for abstract ideas and relationships, and for most occasions in life this is equipment enough. But for the experience that seems to reduce man's individual life to insignificance in relation to a reality that appears to lie wholly beyond it — for this we can only borrow from the language of ordinary life. The question of the "ineffable" experience is raised more than once in these discussions, most explicitly in the last. It is paradoxical that so many people have felt compelled to write at such great length about experiences they begin by describing as indescribable. The essential paradox, though, is that it is in these moments when he can "transcend humanity" that man feels himself to be most truly human.

The real problem, then, is not only one of language. There seems to be built into this kind of experience an essential element that cannot be described without self-contradiction in any language. Ideas like space, time and individuality which hitherto had helped us to make sense of life now come to be felt as limitations to our understanding of it; or rather as concepts only to be fully understood by a comprehension of each held simultaneously in tension with its opposite. Another paradoxical characteristic of such experience is that it is frequently encountered in the most trivial or familiar situations in life. Like Francis Thompson's ladder of angels, set between Heaven and Charing Cross, the experience may invite infinite exploration, but it must also be grounded in the here and now. It may be that the study of religious experience should not stop short of exploring the higher rungs, but one thing should perhaps today have priority, and that is to show that there are absolutely no circumstances in life, however commonplace or undignified, in which such moments of truth may not occur.

These discussions, then, ramble pretty widely over a fair range of human experience. They took place at intervals over several years, in a fairly informal atmosphere, usually after supper in my house. Though each of the participants has had the last word on his own contribution, neither they nor I have made any serious attempt to polish them up, or present a text that will stand as a reasoned and consistent exposition of any particular point of view. I hope that something of the spark of spontaneous encounter still comes through, and that the result will be stimulating and suggestive to others interested in the study of this elusive subject. Some speak from within a particular religious tradition, and were concerned, or were invited, to say how that tradition relates to contemporary experience and to the questions that, to us, that experience seems to raise. Others start from a more individual point of view, and bring their own experience to bear on these questions. And obviously there is a considerable overlap; there is no clear-cut line to be drawn between these two groups.

A few words about each of the named participants are to be found at the end of the book. In the text they are distinguished only by a different typeface from their questioners, who, under the anonymity of italics, include quite a large number of our friends and associates whom we were fortunate to have with us from time to time.

Perhaps I should add an editorial caution here, to say that the views and attitudes underlying some of the questions do not necessarily represent those of any member of our research staff. The variety of viewpoints did in fact enliven these encounters in all sorts of ways (some of which do not find their way into print). I should like to thank most warmly all those who took part: not only those who submitted with such good humour and resilience to our questioning, but all the many others, too numerous to list by name, who joined us on one occasion or another. Two however I must mention. The first is Sir Alister Hardy, who was not only invariably present but who made a unique and characteristic contribution that no anonymity can wholly conceal. The other is my wife, who besides playing a full part in the argument was largely responsible for the convivial atmosphere in which these most enjoyable meetings took place.

EDWARD ROBINSON

1

Christopher Bryant

We began here with the idea of surveying as wide a range as possible of experience that might possibly be regarded as religious. We didn't confine ourselves to those who expressed particular beliefs, though of course people with a Christian background of some sort do predominate.

I find it difficult to understand how far you can have any religious experience without any prior belief: whatever belief you have colours your experience. Without any belief you might not have very much experience.

But there are some experiences which leave those who have them in a state of total incomprehension: they just don't know what has hit them. The experience seems to come out of the blue, to people who have no beliefs in that area at all. They find such experiences very difficult to describe, or to communicate. Still an experience of that kind does tend to remain an isolated phenomenon in a person's life, unless it gets translated, unless it gets fitted in to some credal background, either arising out of it or already present.

I think this is largely true. It's difficult to know what to make of experiences which come out of the blue. It's rather like dreams. Some of these experiences may be like waking dreams, which are not so very different from ordinary dreams except that your critical faculties are more aware and you are able to judge them better.

William James argued that experience was primary and belief secondary — it was what man formulated as the result of having had the experience; the content of the belief was therefore secondary. I don't think this is a fair deduction from the evidence. I don't think you can simply say that the experience is the vital thing and that belief is merely a man's construction from it.

I would agree very much with that. Your belief at least partly gives rise to the experience; not wholly, but partly. And experience will lead one to take certain actions. I think of faith as having four elements: *belief, venture* (that is, putting your belief into practice), *trust,* and *experience.* Faith is more important than experience, which is only part of it.

But may not some experience be prior to faith?

Yes, I think so. I think all our religious ideas are filtered to us through our experience of people. It's very difficult for someone who has grown up without having had any trust in anybody to realise what trust in God means. I do think people have experience of God long before they hear the word "God", through the love of their parents. There's a caring, a warmth, a strength surrounding you, which as a baby you don't think of as God, but it is some divine thing; and later when you are old enough to have some doctrinal teaching you can interpret it; you have had the experience already, and your teaching interprets it.

A very common type of experience described to us as occurring in childhood is one of what some would call "nature mysticism": a sense of oneness with the surroundings. This has no sort of credal anchorage at all; it doesn't arise from any kind of belief as far as one can see, or any kind of religious background. It just comes. This does seem to be a kind of pure experience, antecedent to any belief.

Of course belief and a definite creed aren't quite the same thing. You can have a belief that the world is a good place before you can speak.

You can have a feeling.

Well, yes. One thing I feel strongly is that the world is a very mysterious place. To some extent we have lost this sense of mystery through the efforts of science, which tries to reduce the mystery to things we can measure and classify and so on; and we forget, what every child knows, that the world is somehow a mystery. I think that some childhood experiences are intensified experiences of mystery. Traditional theologians have always insisted in God being the unknown: it is impossible for us to know what God is in Himself: He is utterly mysterious. They qualify this a bit by saying that He is known through His effects, in creation and so on. And then they are apt to take it all back, in talking of particular doctrines which we know very clearly. It seems to me that this doctrine that God Himself is utterly mysterious should be carried into the way we talk about specific doctrines, which should not be as cut and dried as we often say.

Are you then saying that a child's sense of mystery is a more primitive thing, a truer idea of what God is?

I think that today this sense of mystery is apt to be lost by a concentration on what things are in so far as you can measure them and use them, which is the scientific approach.

Yes, for the last three hundred years we have been worshipping this system of measurement, and losing this sense of mystery. And this is the whole reason why we are starting this inquiry. We are at the moment playing the part of naturalists, not of scientists; we are collecting records which I hope will convince the intellectual world that here is something that is very mysterious, and just as important as what the science of measurement can show us, in other directions. And in connection with what you said about the child-parent relationship: I think perhaps Freud was right, in saying that the idea of God as the loving father in heaven may well be related to the child's feeling for his parents; but it is none the worse for that. It doesn't worry me that it should be so. This that we speak of as God, the mysterium tremendum *or whatever we may call it, is something with which we may still have this devotional relationship.*

Well if we are right in thinking of God as creator, then He is responsible for this parent-child relationship, and it is natural that the relationship of the child to the father should be a kind of model for his relationship with God.

One can take this either way. One can say, with Freud, that God is merely the projection into a different plane of these human feelings, or one can argue that the parent-child relationship is due to the primary relationship with God, that our whole understanding of personality is due to the fact that God as personality is primary. Neither of these views can be verified from a scientific point of view.

I agree. Jung, who at one time had shared Freud's outlook, came to take a diametrically opposite point of view. For Freud God was a father-substitute; for Jung the father was a God-substitute. The God-archetype for Jung was more fundamental than the parent-archetype.

Do you think that the child-parent relationship is strikingly different in any particular way from the relationship between any other mammals and their young? Or would you say that was divine too?

I believe that God is the creator, and therefore I would see the same pattern in the life of other mammals. There is a fundamental similarity, but there is a difference because man has qualities that the other animals haven't: his power to think and choose is much greater, and this does make a certain difference in the relationship between parent and child. It's based on instinct, but also other qualities come in.

What happens to the God-pattern, then, if the parent-child relationship is a very bad one?

When the child-parent relationship is a very bad one it is very difficult for the child when he grows older to have a satisfactory relationship to God. One tries to suggest other models. I'm sometimes inclined to suggest the model of mother, but I'm so much of a Westerner that I hesitate to speak of God as mother, though certain Christian mystics have.

But it has got to be some kind of personal model?

Not necessarily. I think myself that you want to balance personal models with impersonal, like light, or fire or something like that. We need to get away from our anthropomorphisms and belittlings of God, and using such impersonal models may help.

It's very difficult to use models which convey the notions of power or purpose without their becoming excessively personal, perhaps sentimentally personal. Yet how can one convey such ideas without the use of a personal model?

I have a theory that a lot of bad religion is due to either the mother-image or the father-image being exclusively used. Of course in the west we don't use a mother-image, but we read maternal attributes into God. We stress his kindness and love, sometimes to the exclusion of other qualities. Just as a child needs mother and father, we need both images for God. The child has first of all the need for the sense that "mother loves me however bad I am, however naughty and smelly and nasty I am". But once this unconditional love of mother has been really learnt, then it equally needs this demanding love that insists that you are good and behave yourself, which is associated with the love of the father. Some people make God in the image of one who will tolerate anything, like the kind mum who doesn't mind what you do, who will comfort you however wrathful father is. The difficulty about this image is that it is quite incredible in view of the state of the world as it is. Then on the other hand we get this stern father idea, the projection of the Freudian superego; and again this is unacceptable, because all our independence is threatened by a sort of super-policeman over against us. We need a sort of mix-up of both these images. I think that a lot of bad religion comes from having either a sort of wishy-washy God of love without any strength or sternness about Him or on the other hand having a very stern, a very righteous God.

Generally speaking those who write in to us describing a sudden, transforming experience which may be of this "nature-mystical" type feel that they have come to grasp what reality is; they usually speak of it in non-personal terms, but they nearly always speak of it in terms of love. The thing they grasp is that reality is love, and that this is all that matters. This kind of experience seems to be separated both from personal ideas of God and from any kind of belief.

I would suspect that they see this in nature because they have had the experience of being loved from their parents, or they have had religious teaching — perhaps; I wouldn't know about this in all cases — but it has been couched in rather different language, of a father with a white beard, a rather stern sort of person; and this is a breaking in of a new experience of God, I would say, that their teaching hasn't allowed for. It has to break in on them because they haven't been taught it, or they haven't been encouraged to think that way.

But the seeds have been there, you would say.

I believe the seeds have been there because I believe that God is operating everywhere. I believe the seeds are there if they have had any sort of love from their parents.

It seems to me there are two questions here. On the one hand you have the seriously deprived, whose experience has made it very difficult for them to form any adequate conception of God; on the other you have this breaking in from nowhere of a completely new confidence in reality. You will only ruin it all if you try to explain it by saying they got it from somewhere, or that the seeds were sown, because after all, if God is, *then He can break in, against fairly heavy odds. I suppose you've always got to weigh things in the balance.*

I believe very much in the living God: He acts everywhere; and He does use us, normally. But it so often happens that experiences that seem disadvantageous turn out to be, unexpectedly, not so. Just because you are in such desperate straits you may turn for help, and find help, when if you hadn't have been so tried you wouldn't have done so. So I would agree very much that God does break in unexpected ways.

When you say that God uses us "normally", do you mean that all His actions can be interpreted according to psychological laws?

No, I wouldn't think that. I think that all psychological laws, in so far as they are real laws, come from God. But I think we don't understand God. I think *we* are mysterious. In *The Cloud of Unknowing* you are encouraged to think of God, or rather not to think of Him but of a cloud of unknowing, as a sort of symbol that enables the arguing reason to be quiet so that intuition may wake up. I think you get something similar in Buddhist techniques. It does seem to me that in order to apprehend God, or even a human being, you have to confess your ignorance: "Lord, I don't know you." And in the very act of admitting your ignorance you get a kind of knowledge, a kind of awareness. I think this is also true of people. We are apt to categorize people, and say "Oh yes, I know him", and sort of cut them down to size in our own mind. We've got to affirm "No, I don't know him at all, he's a mystery". And in this act of the conscious mind admitting its incapacity it opens itself to unconscious perceptions, or intuitions from the unconscious. I do think that God is absolutely mysterious. Although I would certainly affirm that all psychological laws come from God, and therefore we can to some extent use them as clues, yet God is ultimately mysterious.

This raises the question of the miraculous, doesn't it. Do you believe that God may act in such a way as to break material laws, so that His acts may appear miraculous, or do you think He acts within those laws? And does the same thing apply to psychological laws?

I find it very hard to think that God break His own laws. We may formulate "laws", but is God obliged to obey the "laws" we formulate? These "laws" are merely, as far as we are able to judge, the way things normally happen.

I would say that we discover laws rather than that we formulate them.

Yes.

And that we have by no means discovered all of them.

Yes.

If there is anything in Jung's idea of the collective unconscious, and in the balancing effect of the unconscious, if one has a personal experience of parents which is bad, and one is in this way deprived — if there is anything in Jung's theory, one should be able to find in such cases that the positive stuff that's in the collective will come up, but that it won't be able to take the form that it takes in normal experience; the experience of love, the positive or whatever, will come up in some shape that the person can take, maybe through nature or something. In other words, the stuff that is deep down somewhere which is positive has got to infiltrate through some kind of perceptual framework that one has, and if it can't come through a parental relationship it will take some other form.

I would think so. You have Brother Lawrence who as an eighteen-year-old boy saw a tree in the winter stripped of its leaves, and reflected that presently the tree would put forth bud and leaf and eventually blossom and fruit; and as he reflected he suddenly was filled with a sense of the love and presence of God, which never left him for fifty years. He brought a certain belief, a certain faith to that experience. What the experience actually was I don't know but it was certainly an experience of love. And unless he had had some sort of awareness of God in him, he wouldn't have seen anything in a tree.

I don't know. I think there's something far more primal in this than we suspect. Certainly many people describe it as being so surprising, so totally beyond their previous experience that they don't know what to make of it. To say that they must first of all have a concept of God or some knowledge of God for them to have such an experience doesn't seem to me right.

Conversion experiences, now; they come like a bolt from the blue, but I believe they are always prepared for.

But they are quite a different matter. We have so many of these accounts, you see, that are of experiences from quite early life. It may be of course that some of the people who describe them may in fact have forgotten some even earlier instruction, but they so often describe them as something totally inexplicable, totally primary. Is one to say that they must be based on some kind of previous concept of God?

Christopher Bryant

Some people, of course, would account for them by some theory of reincarnation.

I wouldn't say they are fully accounted for by some previous experience.

But you said that Brother Lawrence could not have had such an idea if it hadn't been for some previous awareness.

He was eighteen at the time; and I think he interpreted it in the way he did because of his, no doubt, Christian upbringing; he believed in God the creator and so on.

Do you think it is a sudden feeling that there's something bigger and other than me, and therefore it can't just come in the shape of a relationship just with a mother or a father; it's a sudden break-through to the immediately personal from something bigger?

Trying to remember my own earliest experiences, I can recall an experience when I was very very young when I was taught to pray; there was a kind of picture of God in heaven. I can't remember a beard or anything like that, but anyhow there was a sort of picture. But the most genuine experience came later, at the seaside, on my own, at Whitstable, a place on the Thames estuary where the tide goes out for about a mile, and there is a great stretch of sand and sea.

Mud, actually.

Well, mud, yes. Anyhow, I enjoyed it enormously; there was a sort of cosmic sense. Of course I didn't think of it at the time; I never thought of it specially, but I enjoyed it. I don't really know if it was exactly a religious experience, but certainly there was a sense of being in touch with a certain vastness. How far I am reading that into it I don't know. And later I used to get a tremendous sense of God in nature, in sunsets and things like that, which leave me completely cold now. I like them, aesthetically, but they don't now give me a specially religious feeling.

Do you feel this as a loss? As some sort of deadening of the sensibilities, if one may speak like that?

I think this is very interesting. I think there is a shift from an awareness of God outside to an awareness of God within. There was a time when I used to love praying before the Blessed Sacrament, the symbol of a presence outside me, and this meant a tremendous lot to me. Now it means absolutely nothing. My belief about it is exactly as it was then, but I have a much bigger realization of God now than I had then, I think. It's different. I think one changes, and I think one probably should change. Whether this is invariably the case I don't know; but it is quite normal for people to project their sense of God onto things outside them to begin with, and as they grow older to find God within them.

You said, "I believe in the living God". Now what is your objective evidence of this? If you stand outside yourself in a sceptical way, as I sometimes try to do myself, what do you say?

I find it very difficult to answer this question, because I have been in the habit of believing in God, of relying on God, for such a long time. I find it extremely difficult to say what grounds I have. I went through a time of turmoil about this. I left off saying my prayers at — I don't know what age, thirteen or fourteen or so; and I went through a painful period of adolescent doubt at seventeen or eighteen, when I was really coming to faith, and that was why it was painful. And curiously enough it was William James' book, *The Varieties of Religious Experience,* that was the intellectual turning point. I may be wrong, but I think that what really affected me was the realization that there was such a thing as religious experience. I hadn't realized this before; that there was something interesting about religion. It wasn't just some dead, utterly boring thing, like going to church which I hated. Anyway, I did go through an agonizing time, asking is there a God or not; and for about three or four months I'd be a believer in the evening, and in the morning I'd wake up an atheist, or an agnostic anyhow; and after a bit I settled down to being more or less a believer. I find it very difficult not to believe now. I can question; but it's very difficult for me now to enter into the atheistic point of view. On this question of evidence, I believe we haven't got complete evidence: we can't prove God's existence; we have to go on probabilities.

But I can look back and I can say thus and thus and thus: here are things that to me point quite clearly. And I can't see any fair explanation of them for myself except a Christian one.

I would find it difficult to point to specific experiences. What convinces me more than specific experiences is the total experience of living on the God-assumption for a long time. I feel more and more convinced of the truth of this. You can say this is just auto-suggestion.

Christopher Bryant

I'm not sure that this is a satisfactory explanation. You can't always auto-suggest yourself when you want to; and I think one's awareness of facts can overthrow suggestions about things which one would like to have. However, getting back to your point, I would say I find it very difficult to point to particular experiences, partly because I'm rather critical of experiences. I mean, many times I have felt very strongly the presence of God, at times of retreat for example, which are times when one is silent, and reflects on religious truth, while reading books and listening to addresses and all that sort of thing; and I have had an overwhelming sense of God's presence then. But the sceptical part of me says, well, this doesn't prove anything really. And I always maintain that the important part of faith is not so much experience, though that comes into it, as much as acting it out, basing your life on it and finding that things tend to confirm it. The real test is "by their fruits" and so on: but one can't judge one's own life in that way, though one can judge other people's to some extent.

When you said that the sense of mystery can be destroyed by attempting too scientific, or pseudo-scientific, an approach, I was thinking of some of the people who feel that it isn't only science that has been the difficulty but also theology, and the church. Their experiences have taken some people into *practising religion or joining some denomination. But other people through their experience have been taken* out, *because they felt there wasn't any real understanding or appreciation of that experience.*

There is something wrong with the church; I wouldn't wish to have to defend everything in the church at all; I should feel very uncomfortable. It does seem to me that there is a great interest in religion today among the young, but very little interest in the church.

Doesn't this bring us back to the question of models? Many people today reject all previous models of God, the supernatural or whatever, and believe, indeed find, that, by emptying their minds and practising meditation of one kind or another, something happens. This is done in a purely negative way, without any model at all. They claim to be able to reach new levels of consciousness, in fact to acquire a kind of knowledge, in this way. Do you think one must have a model of some kind?

I am inclined to think that the people who most benefit by a kind of negative way, by emptying the mind and so on, are those who have had some previous discipline in a more positive way. *The Cloud of Unknowing* of course is a great example of the *via negativa,* of the finding of God through the rejection of all images. But it's written for people who have had knowledge of the other, the affirmative way, probably for monks and nuns who have a great deal of set prayers and things like that.

What about the pursuit of higher states of consciousness as an end in itself?

I'm a bit doubtful about this myself. As a means to an end, yes. To me, the end would be union with God's will. I would accept that we should aim at being as conscious as we can of reality, of God.

I read something lately which you wrote on this subject, in which you described how it struck you suddenly, in some cathedral, when someone said to you: "But Christ did not suffer" — it struck you suddenly what a tremendous difference there was between the person for whom the approach *was all important, the meditation itself, and the Christian, for whom the* end *is what matters most.*

Yes, I remember that case. I think perhaps I wasn't fair to the chap; very often people are much better than their theories. I don't think he was really as escapist as it sounded. But it seemed to me that for him meditation was a means of getting tranquillity of mind and escaping from the world's problems; that is how it seemed to me at the time. This is a criticism that I have heard made of some eastern religions, that what they regard as ends the Christian would regard as means to an end, means to a union with God which would express itself in union with his fellow men.

The apophatic tradition in the church seems to help a lot here. One must never say: "God is just like my feeling for my mother" and so on. God is not *just like such feelings; He is so much more.*

Yes. In fact, any model is found to be inadequate if you take it too seriously. A model is a help; we can't do without models, but they become idols if you treat them as the *one* way. All words about God can become idolatrous unless we are prepared to say, "Ah, yes, but God is really much more than that". This is very orthodox Christian theology, that we can't really know God as He is, and that all our words, the truest things we can say about Him, are pointers to a mystery.

Christopher Bryant

There is often a great aridity about people who remain, as it were, "nature mystics" all their lives, and never get beyond that to anything else.

I can't help wondering whether or how far a good deal of "nature mysticism" isn't a kind of craving for a mother goddess which in the west we haven't got, because our way of thinking of God is too masculine. We think of "mother nature", don't we. Not that this is consciously the reason why people are drawn to nature; but it is a way of apprehending the divine other than through a father model.

Perhaps there are some people who today are drawn to some form of nature mysticism through reaction to too personal a model of God. There is a definite reaction against moralizing, the association of moral demands with the divine.

Yes, you see, your mother is not associated with the superego; it is your father as a rule. I'm not saying that mothers are necessarily more immoral than fathers.

Amoral!

Well, we don't associate mothers with do's and don't's in the same way as we do fathers.

I should have thought that nature mysticism is not so much to be associated with feelings for mothers or fathers as with what Otto called the sense of the numinous; it is something similar to what one may feel in a sacred building, this sense of the mysterium tremendum *but felt in a slightly different way. I don't think it is exactly the same. William James at one point says that this sense of the numinous is exactly the same as the feeling one may have in a pine forest or in certain mountains. I don't think it is; but it is similar, a consciousness of something that I am sharing with something that is beyond myself, which I call God, or the transcendental element. I've never associated it with a mother- or father-concept at all. But I've never prayed to nature; prayer is I think a personal approach, towards a loving father.*

Yes.

One needs to have some experience of something beyond one's own mother and father, because you feel you know your own parents so well that there's no mystery left there — though this isn't true, but it's our feeling that it is so.

Yes I think we do need something impersonal; I think possibly this idea of the mother is something of a red herring.

Could you say what you feel about what William James called "the religion of healthy-mindedness"? There seem to be people who are able to feel that everything has a rosy glow and that they long to give to others this feeling that everything is all right and that the world is all good and so on. They may speak of problems, but they do not seem really to face them. I sometimes find it hard to sympathize with such people.

Well we are each of us located in a particular vantage-point by our own experience, and therefore we can only see what can be seen by a person who has had that experience. One can't say what is the best place to be in. Sometimes the very worst experiences do produce the most extraordinarily valuable insights. A friend of mine who is a psychiatrist has made a study of St. John of the Cross; he says he was a depressive, but that he overcame his handicap and was able to write his great works because he had been through this experience of depression and came through it triumphantly. But all his works are coloured by it: he couldn't have seen things as he did if he hadn't been a depressive.

I sometimes think all sensitive people are depressives.

He meant in the medical sense, I think. Then again, I'm sure the healthy-minded person has a certain perception of things which is denied to the rather more morbid type, like many of us; and it may well be that he has a certain insight which comes from his happy disposition.

You are a member of a religious order, in which community is a most important element. One of the most striking characteristics of almost all the experiences which we have had described to us is that they are largely individual: they concern the personal ideas and personal development of those who had them. Do you think there are certain types of experience, certain levels of experience, which cannot really be achieved or appreciated except in some form of community, or in some kind of close contact with other people?

I would think that this very well may be so. I think it may equally be so that certain experiences cannot be had except in solitude; and of course the hermit life is one form of religious experience, and the monk hasn't got the experience of being married, and so on. I would think that wherever you are your experience will enable you to have certain perceptions, certain realizations that somebody in a different situation won't have. I was trying to think as you were speaking whether there was anything specific in being a member of a religious community in one's experience. I suppose there's the experience of corporate worship, and of the support in being one of a community. I think there is a real support which you gain from belonging to a community of faith, where we all, roughly, believe the same things. I have no doubt I disagree violently with some people, but all the same basically we have a great deal in common, and I think this is a great support, especially nowadays when one is living in a society which doesn't give great importance to spiritual values. It may be that in a community you can be more relaxed in your faith, less on the defensive, than you would if you were living outside.

Living in a loving, accepting community, which one hopes communities of choice would be, would surely enlarge one's feeling of the loving nature of the transcendent. It would be terrible if one felt one could not modify earlier impressions of mother or father by any sort of later loving experience. One would hope that living in a loving relationship with other people could lead to a more understanding love of God.

I would think that where a community was a good one, where there was a real loving relationship, this is bound to affect you.

William James was very much concerned with religion in solitude; he almost says what Whitehead says, that religion is what a man does with his solitude. This is very different from Durkheim's view, that religion is essentially a social thing.

William James was more of the protestant tradition, but you can see something of the same thing in monasticism. The first monks were solitaries, and then they gathered themselves into families. Always in monasticism there are these two different ideas which both pull against each other and work together: the desert, and the family. The original monks went into the desert to be alone, but they discovered this wasn't a good thing; they went queer; so they gathered themselves into little families of monks, centred round some spiritual guide. Even in a religious community you get times of silence. In my community we have the cell, which is the place where one sleeps and may work; but we don't normally have conversations in our cells; they are places where one is alone. Not all communities have the same practice; but there is always a certain solitariness within a community. I think you have got to have both these ideas, of the desert and the family, in a healthy community. I believe that even in a family an individual must be allowed to be himself, and must not be bulldozed into conformity, if he is to be happy.

We do, of course, have a number of accounts of experience coming in from people whom one might call casualties of our society, people who have difficulty in relating to others, who haven't perhaps got a very strong sense of identity. They often describe the feeling that something has happened that enables them to be less solitary, and say they are better able to get on with other people as a result.

One gets a number of strange people, of course, who think that the solution to all their problems is to become a religious. I don't think it ever is. I think one of the qualifications if one wants to live in a religious community is to be able to form relationships with other people. If you can't do that, you can't be very happy in a religious community.

You presumably find within the community that there is a sharing of experience as well as of belief, a sort of hitting it off with other people because they experience what they would say was the same Lord. Would you say that this sense of fellowship comes not only from your all having the same beliefs, but also from your sharing of experience, so that your conversation becomes much more illuminating: you can talk about things, areas of experience, about which it is much more difficult to talk with others?

I think there's something in this, though I don't think we do talk a great deal to each other about our experiences actually. Curiously, one of the times when one feels most at one with everybody is in our times of retreat. My community has the rather unusual custom of having every year two periods, a week in one case and over a week in the other, in which we are silent; we don't have ordinary conversation at all. And it seems that in this time of silence we are very close to each other; there is an extraordinary sense of fellowship that develops at these times. Of course, people vary enormously temperamentally as to how much silence they like. There are some people who adore silence; other people find it difficult to be silent for a couple of hours on end, but I imagine that sort of person wouldn't find his vocation in our community.

There's an interesting observation by Ivan Illich in his book Celebration of Awareness*: he says that if one wants to understand a language and not just its words one has to learn to listen to the silences, and that until one has learnt to listen, and understand what people mean by the gaps between the words, one hasn't really got the language.*

This is very interesting, because it brings one back to this sense of mystery. You have got to listen, to make yourself aware; you have got to stop talking, to stop thinking, in order to have all your antennae working, so as to pick up what is there.

Do you think that if one remains silent long enough, consistently enough, one may be able to recover what in psychic terms would be described as a capacity for telepathy, especially within a community?

I should think this is very likely to be so, for some people at any rate.

This reminds me of a conversation I once had with one of the sisters in an enclosed contemplative community. A lot of the time there is spent in silence; but when they come into the chapel for liturgical worship, they know immediately if something is wrong with somebody. It is as though silence does make for some kind of extra awareness.

Yes. From a psychological point of view the effect of silence must be to help one become aware of what is going on inside oneself, and in other people too, because we interact.

Would you say there was any connection between telepathy and intercessory prayer?

I think there must be. I have found great resistance among my fellow believers to this idea, because they think one is somehow taking God out of it, as it were. I cannot in the least see why this should be so. I am positive that intercession does affect people, mysteriously though, because there is no kind of one-to-one relationship between your prayer and any effect. And as on other grounds I am sure there is such a thing as telepathy, I should be very much surprised if there wasn't a connection between the two.

If one does dream about someone whom one hasn't seen for ages, or something else extraordinary happens, this might be a signal to say "pray"; it may be that they need one, so to speak, to bounce them back to God.

Yes. I have an interpretation of one of the strange sayings of Christ: "Whatsoever ye ask believing it shall be done unto you". I have an idea that the prayers that God will answer are the prayers that He has Himself inspired; you can only pray this way if you are inspired. I think we are often inspired to pray for particular things or for particular people. I find it very difficult to pray other than for a person. I bring a person before God in prayer; I don't tell God what He's to do or anything like that. My faith in God and my remembrance of that person come together. Dorothy Kerin, in her book *The Living Touch*, tells a story of how she had a feeling that she ought to go to church to communion one day, and on her way to church she had a very strong impression that she was to pray for three people who were ill. When she got to church, in the service she looked up, and the whole altar and everything seemed to be hidden in a purple haze, which as she looked took the form of a cross. Points of red appeared just where our Lord's hands and feet would have come on the cross. She prayed for these three people; and presently the whole thing disappeared. Later that day she heard that these three people had got well. I would think that somehow or other, whether intuitively or telepathically, she was told to pray for these people, became aware of their need, and the prayer was answered. I don't understand it. But I would say she was inspired, or led, to pray for the thing which the spirit of God wanted to come about.

You said she had a strong impression. Do you think one should cultivate a sort of receptivity to strong impressions of this kind?

I think if such an impression comes it may well be a thing you should act on. Actually I find intercession rather a difficult thing; very little of my prayer really is intercession. I commend everything and everybody to God together; but occasionally if I have been asked to pray for some particular person I do; and also one occasionally gets an impression that somebody needs prayer.

But the cultivation of this kind of thing — living on hunches if you like — can become quite obsessional.

Yes, I think it can. I get a little bit worried when people live too much by intuition. A friend of mine who had been in India told of a man whom he would sometimes see in the road with one leg in the air; he was waiting for inspiration as to whether he was to move forward or not. You can get so used to waiting on guidance that you can't do anything at all.

But there are a number of people whose lives are spent in a devotion to the service of God, for whom this kind of experience must be very common; deliberately giving a large part of their time to prayer, and being totally dependent on God to supply their daily needs.

It does seem that where people live with this tremendous faith, trusting God to intervene in their daily affairs, extraordinary things happen. Look at that book, *The Cross and the Switchblade.* Your whole project is going to collapse unless you get, let's say, a hundred and five pounds by a certain date; a hundred pounds comes in, and you think you've missed it; then the five pounds turns up. This sort of thing happens again and again in these stories. Whether it's telepathy — whether people are being induced by telepathic means to fork out the money, I don't know. But extraordinary things do happen. Where people do base their policies and plans on faith, venturing when they haven't got any assurance that it's safe to do so, amazing things happen. In a way, it's carrying this principle of "unknowing" into a different dimension — being "unknowing" about the future, going forward without knowing where you're going to get the money. Until you are prepared to get onto the ice when you have no proof that the ice will bear your weight, though you have a certain amount of reason for thinking it will — when you do that, you find things happen.

Could this be described, not in personal terms, as for example getting something organised by some supernatural power, but rather in terms of something more like the collective unconscious, as though we could tap a level at which all people are, so to speak, subterraneously joined up, so that other people might become unconsciously aware of one's needs?

I would think something like this happens. When you really trust God in this practical way, it is as though you are trusting people, and people, somehow, intuitively, come to your rescue.

What are your views on astrology?

Very sceptical. I've had some doubt cast on my scepticism, but I couldn't say more. I've taken the view that astrology is a projection of an awareness of certain determinants which are really within us, onto the stars. There are real determinants of our destiny, but they are within us, and possibly at work in ordinary mundane forces. But I find it very difficult to think that the movements of the stars can have any affect on us. However, people whose intelligence I respect don't take this view, and I wonder if I am not being a bit too sceptical; but I cannot see how it can happen.

But some astrologers would argue that it isn't exactly a causal connection between the position of the signs of the zodiac and what happens, but that there is some way of interpreting factors on earth in accordance with what is going on elsewhere.

What you are saying suggests to me very much the kind of thing I said before, that is that there are real determinants within us and that we project them on to other things and then read them; like the *I Ching,* which I don't understand at all, this may be a method of getting at things which are really in you unconsciously; the same with dowsers, and these people who use pendulums. These are presumably ways of getting at information which they already know unconsciously, but which the conscious mind cannot reach.

Perhaps there's an inner harmony that reflects an outer one, each individual being a sort of microcosm of the universe.

I would rather put it this way: we are all created by God, and there must be something God-like about everything that God has made.

If I might pursue this question just a little further, there is perhaps an alternative way of looking at this question of divination, whether by the stars, by the Tarot, or by tea-leaves. One may say that the relevant information is in oneself in some unconscious form. Or one may say that since the whole of the universe is operating on some vast plan or pattern, so that every element in it, every minutest particle, is related to every other, therefore if one could correctly read the relationship between any two or three particles of the universe, we should find implied in that relationship the pattern of the whole. If we could properly understand even a small part of the universe, some small corner of the creative process, that understanding, if it were complete, would give an insight into the rest.

I find it hard to think of everything as predetermined; so I would be inclined not to accept that way of looking at things. I find it simpler to say that anything may act as a symbol which awakens some deeper awareness. Things may be interconnected, they no doubt are interconnected, but on such a vast scale we couldn't possibly work it out.

2

Lev Gillet

In our original appeal people were asked to write an account of any experience in which they felt they had been influenced by some power either beyond or partly beyond themselves, and to tell us of the effect such experience had had on their lives. We have as a result an enormous variety of accounts, ranging from the most sensational descriptions of the supernatural and occult, visitations from the dead and encounters with flying saucers to a more traditional type of religious experience. How would you approach such a collection?

I think each case should be regarded as different, and should be studied and analysed very carefully for itself.

Having done that one finds certain common features. What would you expect to find of particular interest?

It would depend on your conception of a religious phenomenon. I have my own conception of course.

Could you tell us what criteria you would apply?

I think you have a religious phenomenon when you have, firstly, the awareness of a reality which transcends you: something bigger than yourself, something beyond your own limits. And secondly, although it is transcendent, it must in some way be immanent to yourself, you must find it in yourself. And thirdly, between these two expressions of a supreme reality (which I shall not define at all now) there is a possibility of dynamic exchange. You receive something from it, and you give something to it. That is my conception of a religious phenomenon. And this applies to many cases where you don't have a God. You may consider sex, for instance, as this supreme reality both transcendent and immanent. This might be a kind of religion. You might consider society, or the cosmos, taken in a scientific sense. Or you can consider it as a personal or supra-personal reality — God.

But in what sense can sex, society or the cosmos be transcendent?

Well, let us take the case of the Freudian psychologist. He may consider the libido to be a power transcendent to himself and yet immanent in every man, and constituting the supreme reality: something corresponding to the *élan vital* of Bergson.

But isn't this a bit of wishful thinking? He's actually projecting it and regarding it as transcendent because he wants to have something which is actually beyond himself, isn't he?

I am not judging him. I am only interested to know whether *for him* it has a transcendent value or not.

Would you then say that everybody is in some sense religious?

I don't know; I'm not sure; there may be people who are not at all. But I suppose that most people are, in many thousand different ways.

How then would you recognize a non-religious person? Would it be someone for whom there is no meaning to existence?

Yes; or a man who would not acknowledge anything beyond his own reality, bodily or mental. Take a Marxist: I don't consider him as not religious. Marxism is quite a theology. Dialectical materialism, firstly in so far as it is materialism, is dogmatic; and secondly, "dialectical" implies this kind of cosmic, universal structure.

You can argue from this that anyone who feels any kind of meaning in life is religious.

Maybe; but I think there are many people who have no quest at all for meaning: people who are not interested, who do not acknowledge or recognize such a need. They live from day to day, never asking questions.

But are there really people like this, people who demand no meaning at all?

I have met quite a number of them. At first I was under an illusion: I thought these people really had some inner anxiety but didn't know how to express it, or were not aware of it. I have changed this view now because I have met, in London, quite a few men and women who are certainly not asking any questions; they do not feel any need for meaning, they have no interest in it. Seemingly, their experience is just a reaction to the course of events and circumstances as they come.

Would you say that this attitude can survive a crisis in their lives? I am interested by the number of people who write to us telling of the effects of crises of one kind or another, and of how, until they were confronted with things that demand some meaning — bereavement and so on — they really did not search for any meaning. Would you say that the kind of people you describe have never been brought up against problems that demand something deeper than mere day-to-day existence?

Let me tell you of a very strange experience I had last year. Last year, at this very time, in March, I was very, very ill. I was dying. For about a week I was unconscious, and delirious. On the one hand I was saying senseless things to the people around me. But the whole time there was the development within me of a kind of dialectic, of which I was aware, and which had great continuity. It was the development of a dream, or a vision, which I will tell you about now.

On the first day of my illness I had been paying a visit to a Persian woman who had a spastic child. I visited her with my own doctor. And I saw that spastic child moving on the bed, and uttering groans, and trying to make movements but not able to co-ordinate them. He was simply holding a little bottle of milk, and groaning, and groping for something. And then some visitors arrived, also a Persian family. The situation was rather awkward: the mother was annoyed, and it was evident that she would have liked them to go away. And suddenly the child, the spastic child, seemed to become aware of things, and got up somehow, and said "Mama, kawa!" It meant that the child was aware that you offer coffee to any guest; he was reminding his mother that she should offer coffee to them. What was striking, deeply moving, was to see the child suddenly coming out of his own frontiers, his prison as a spastic child, and getting an altruistic interest in these people. I was extremely impressed.

The following night I began to become extremely ill; I began to lose consciousness. And then I had a dream — or did I see it in some imaginary way? — I don't know. I saw myself on a very white plain, during a dark night; I was lying on the earth. To the right and left I could see no light whatever, no houses, nothing. But coming out of the earth here and there, like worms rising, there were little spastic beings. And some of them were saying the word "coffee" ("kawa" in Persian); and each with a very little light, like glow-worms. Suddenly I had the impression that I had a vision of the whole universe: that our universe is one in which everyone is to some extent a spastic child. Everybody is moving according to his own spasm, which may be ambition, money, sex, anything. Everyone is a prisoner of his own spasm, like that spastic child. But it happens that suddenly some of them become aware of realities outside of themselves, and begin to ask for coffee for other people.

And for me this was a kind of dialectic which developed during a whole week in my subconscious life, while I was delirious in the eyes of other people. And it seemed to me that the whole universe was like this. And the meaning of any progress in the world was that we should help all these spastic beings around ourselves to become able, at some time, to ask for coffee for others. And this was going on for a whole week, with developments which I shall not enter into now. There was a dialectic sequence in all this.

Now I think that what you said, that there are people, who, unless they come to a crisis, are not aware of this, is right. Yes; they are spastic, moving only somewhat mechanically, until the moment comes when suddenly their eyes are opened and they become aware of other people.

This suggests that our natural state is not to be aware of meaning, and that we all have to be raised out of this.

But, according to my own conception, which is purely individual and which I cannot prove or disprove, I think that the spastic child could never become able to think of coffee for other people if it was not suggested, or given, by something or somebody that is transcendent to him: what a Christian would call grace.

How would you delimit this that is called the transcendent? We have among our correspondents great numbers of people who say, "We have found meaning, this is our religious experience." One cannot approach it entirely without preconceptions, without values of one's own. We have to ask how the transcendent power is to be recognized; and also whether influences of this nature can be evil as well as good.

For me there was no question about it: I had come to this interpretation of the dream because I already had my own religious convictions. And these for me are connected with a personal or suprapersonal power; one with which, or with whom, I think I have had personal contact at certain times of my life — the deciding moments of my life. I have had, in my entirely personal, intimate life, first a feeling of presence, of a given, suprapersonal presence. This was with me for a whole hour in an extremely intense way, taking hold of me, making me cry without any cause, overwhelming me completely. That happened to me on the shore of Lake Galilee. And many times in my life when I have asked for guidance, asking for an answer in concrete terms, this has been given to me, in words: words innerly spoken, without a sound, but in a way which left me in no doubt about the superhuman origin of those answers. I have some criteria which allowed me to discriminate such words from other words, purely human words.

In this feeling of presence, did you feel that anybody was near you in this particular spot?

I didn't see anybody; it didn't take any configuration, any shape, any form. It was simply the presence of a reality to whom I could reach out, and who could reach out to me; and who was associated in my mind with the person of Jesus. Perhaps it was because it happened to me on the shore of the Lake of Galilee: perhaps it was the surrounding influence, the landscape and the recollections associated with the Lake of Galilee in the gospel. But it was so powerful that I suddenly saw that the intentions I had had to go to Jerusalem were quite useless. What I had seen, what I felt, surpassed anything that I could have done in Jerusalem. I had immediately to return to Europe, and nothing else.

Have you had other instances of this sense of presence?

Yes, I have had many instances, but this one, and also the kind of dream about the spastic people, were the most striking. About that dream — the impact on me was this: if I wanted to see the spastic children emerging from the earth I could do this only if I myself was lying completely flat on the ground, losing all feeling of self-importance, realizing that everything I do, writing, speaking to people, is of no importance whatever. The only thing for me is to be able to lie down. And then I may be able to see these spastic people emerging. And the only thing I can do is to help such people as them.

How would you relate these dream experiences and the sense of presence which you felt to the kind of experiences which other people would call purely psychic?

I have no psychic experience whatever. These things are quite foreign to me.

Many people write in to us, describing what really seems to them to be a religious experience, when they have seen a light, or lights, or their surroundings lit up; and this is combined with joy, and sometimes awe. Why should this be so common?

I think that it is a very common phenomenon of all religions. I myself, for instance, have very often a feeling not of an external light but of a kind of inner illumination, something bright, associated with the name of Jesus. I have practised quite a lot what the Orthodox call the Jesus prayer, which consists simply of the repetition of the name of Jesus. This experience of the name of Jesus can become something pervading, and can bring a kind of inner light: you feel enveloped with an inner light, which you cannot describe.

How would you defend this against the criticism of the sceptic that this is just a technique, and that the content is irrelevant? Any philosophy you like could be the context for this kind of experience.

I wouldn't deny it. I think it is quite possible it has a psychological origin. But I would also say that I don't dissociate Jesus from Mohammed, or from Buddha or Krishna, or from many other divinities, Isis or Aphrodite. I think many people have genuine contacts with Jesus under other names, other forms.

And they would take the same attitude as you, presumably?

A Hindu certainly would.

You say you have no psychic experience. But what would you say to someone who described your experiences as psychic? Your sense of presence for example?

I wouldn't say anything. Neither his assertion nor mine can be proved. I would leave it at that.

One of our great problems is that it is very difficult to distinguish between what some people would dismiss as psychic and what others would give great value to and call religious. And yet the core of the experiences in many cases seems very similar. What seems to be the religious element is the way in which people react, the way they receive it or respond to it.

These are things which may be shared, or not shared. If a person doesn't share the experience, it is useless to talk about it. In these matters there is no verification in the scientific sense. Where there is no measurement there is no verification, and you cannot apply measurement to these things. It is a purely qualitative domain, without any possibilities of quantitative research.

Then you would say that unless you can produce results in quantitative form your work is not scientific?

There was a time when I was working in the laboratory of Experimental Psychology in Geneva with Claparède. On the door of his laboratory he had put these words of Lord Kelvin, the British physicist: "If you are able to express what you speak of by a number then you know something about it. If not, then you know nothing about it, and what you say is of no value whatever."

Would you still accept this point of view?

Certainly, from a scientific point of view. I make in my mind an absolute wall between what is susceptible to scientific research (what is measurable) and what is not. There is no bridge between the quantitative and the qualitative.

Is one more real than the other? Or do you not judge?

It is not for me to judge. I am a perfect agnostic in one way, and a perfect believer in another.

Are you not open to the charge of compartmentalization, of thinking in terms of two worlds which you do not allow to come in contact with each other?

No, I shouldn't say that. I simply say that I do not dare to say that I know, if I cannot prove experimentally what I know.

Then the only kind of psychology you would accept as scientific is a kind of behaviouristic psychology?

No, I reject behaviourism as I reject psychoanalysis. For me, the only kind of proved scientific psychology is psycho-statistics.

One could argue against Lord Kelvin that numbers have in fact no more than mythical significance.

Numbers are the only practical way in which to apply knowledge to life. Without numbers there is no scientific knowledge, no scientific technique. I don't believe in a mystique of numbers, not at all.

I think Kelvin also said that he could only really understand a theory if he could construct a model.

That is imagination. That sentence has no value for me whatsoever. What has value is number, the reality. The model has no reality; it is a fiction of the mind. Models in science may change every twenty years: number remains.

But a model is useful in communicating your ideas to someone else.

Yes, in a purely empirical way.

I think one can argue that numbers too are merely a model, that any scientific description is perhaps a model in a different language: one which is more useful in some ways; you can use it for control or prediction. But it is still a model: it does not bring us any nearer to what is really there.

I don't understand this conception of "what is really there". A deep impression was produced in me by something that happened in a botanical laboratory. I was trying to draw what I saw through the microscope. The teacher came to see what everyone was doing. I was drawing cells; but instead of leaving intervals between the cells I was making them quite contiguous. And the teacher said to me, "What do you think you are doing?" I said, "I am trying to draw these cells." "Not at all", he said, "you are doing metaphysics." These words have remained with me, and have had enormous educative influence on me.

What did he mean by them?

He meant that I was drawing something that was not a physical reality. The intervals between the cells were the reality, but I was drawing the cells touching, which was therefore not physical reality, therefore not physics; therefore metaphysics, speculation.

Did he mean you had allowed your perception to be influenced by a metaphysical theory?

No, I don't think he went so far. I think in his mind metaphysics was one of the worst qualifications. It was just that I was drawing something that I did not see.

You said just now that you didn't accept the conception of "what is really there". But at the beginning you spoke of religious experience as experience of a transcendent reality.

Excuse me, I dislike the words "religious experience". I think they are the cause of great confusion, and I blame William James for having introduced such an idea. So try to find some other words. There are a few words I would like to eliminate from the dictionary, such as the words "religious experience", or the word "mysticism."

Could I define religious experience as experience of a religious phenomenon, in other words, of something which is the proper object of our religious interest?

The word "phenomenon" is quite sufficient — "that which appears". What is behind the appearance? I don't know; quantitatively, scientifically, I don't know.

But you have criteria for saying, "I have experienced this; I am now in 'the religious domain'."

I may say that this is the domain of religious phenomena; but, considered from the outside, I think that an atheistic sociologist or psychologist could agree with me on the definition of a religious phenomenon.

You don't think it's necessary to have a religious interest oneself, to be sensitive to something before one can recognize what is significant about it? I don't think an atheist has sufficient interest in the domain of religion to see the significant features of a religious phenomenon.

I know psychologists of religion who are atheists, and who are very interested in mystical phenomena and so on.

And are they qualified to interpret them correctly?

Yes, because they have a scientific mind. I don't care for interpretation very much; I care for description.

But if you describe a phenomenon as religious, surely this word has an interpretative value?

It has a conventional meaning only. I dislike also the words "religion" and "religious". Like the word "mysticism", "religion" has no place in the Bible.

You are ending up in a purely phenomenological position. You say, "I don't ask for an interpretation of these experiences; all I shall do is just approach them all."

Yes, exactly.

But this seems to be rather reductionistic. What is important to the person who has had the experience is his interpretation of it.

I am unable to give interpretation of it. I can only try to grope, to see my way at a given moment.

Then how can you evaluate the experience of other people?

I don't evaluate the experience of other people.

Would you say that this is a scientific attitude?

Yes, exactly. The word "value" has no place in science.

Where do values come from then?

I have no values, probably.

You don't have values?

I don't think so. I have reactions.

Then you think the principles of human conduct are purely relative to the moment?

Now that is a question about my personal ethics.

Yes, but isn't this linked with the whole question of value?

I don't know. I hate the word "value". I hate all these philosophical terms. I may speak of guidance, perhaps; I know what that means; I may know what I should do in particular cases. Or even of love, which is a terrible word.

Are you saying that these things are all intuitive, that it's no good sitting down and trying to work out a system?

I don't know what is "intuitive", although I was a pupil of Bergson in my youth. But I believe there can be this conviction, which has nothing to do with science, that there is an inner light, given by God. I speak of it in the Quaker way.

And in the end the only valid guidance is just what anybody gets, as their own individual experience?

There are no two cases which are alike. There can be no absolute values having the same strength for two different people. Though I quite admit a state must have regulations.

When St. John said "you must try the spirits", to see which are good and which are evil, didn't he imply you must have some criterion of judgement?

Yes, I have criteria.

Where do they come from?

They come from God, I think.

Doesn't this lead to a position where everyone can say, "I have my own intuitive values, my own guidance, and it's as good as yours"?

I certainly think you always have a right to say, "my guidance is as good as yours." If it's really guidance it is as good as the guidance of anybody else. There is no guidance common to two different people.

But our knowledge of God is imperfect, and each of us interprets the will of God according to his own experience. You would surely say that some people are nearer to the mind of God than others?

Certainly. But God has a way of acting differently according to each individual. And I would absolutely reject as a horrible heresy — in so far as I am a heresy-hunter, which I am — the idea that God loves some people better than others. I would say there is nothing quantitative in God; there is no plus or minus in God. Don't quantify God. Don't quantify the love of God. The love of God is a kind of atmospheric pressure which is bearing on everybody equally. The only difference is that there are people who open themselves up to this pressure, while others close themselves. But it is the same undivided, total, divine, absolute love surrounding everybody, speaking to everybody, acting on everybody.

And a Hitler, a Stalin, is supremely closed to this; is that so?

Certainly. They have been surrounded by the same pressure of divine love as any great saint but they have closed themselves.

As a pupil of Bergson's, could you tell us what his approach was to questions of this kind? He would surely have given validity to the experience of other people.

Yes, very much so.

More than you would?

No. I have the greatest respect for the genuine experience of other people. As Bergson said, when you want to know about a subject you go to a specialist. If I want to know about the reality of spiritual things I go straight away to the mystics, to the saints, to the people who have visions or ecstasies. They know about it, and I don't; I must get information from them. If I want some electric repairs done in my house, I go for an electrician.

Then you would say there can be some value in the study of other people's religious experience?

The religious experience of another person may open tremendous landscapes to me, tremendous visions, new visions. And I shall always be grateful to those people whose visions have enlarged mine.

This would include William James?

Well, I have very complex feelings about William James.

Many people have felt grateful to James because through his work he opened their minds to the possibility of religious experience.

Yes, his book had a tremendous influence. But I wonder if it has not simply aroused an interest in this question. Has it led to a wider belief in the validity of such experiences? Scientifically it is very interesting: religiously it is not interesting at all. The only religious question would be: did James' book create in the people who read it more love towards God, and towards their neighbours?

He created in many people, I am sure, who were not previously ready to take these things seriously, a readiness to ask "I wonder whether there is anything in this or not?" And this has started many people on the bottom of a ladder which . .

Yes, probably so. I think his influence may have been very positive.

Now you have introduced some values; you have slipped them in at the back door: positive attitudes, the love of God — why are these things worthwhile?

Oh, because I have been told they are worthwhile, by God.

But what would you say of someone who had had the reverse experience?

I would probably say that he has had a genuine experience, and that God had spoken to him through his conviction which is very different from my own. But there must be some flaw somewhere. But I think that every experience which is genuine, which is immediate, which is sincere, is *true*. I should say that a genuine experience brings a genuine contact with God.

This brings a great richness, but also a supreme disorder, it seems to me.

I am not sure that this universe *is* very well ordered. It is a conception of mine that this universe is not the one which God made: it is an imperfect universe. And that God, my God, is a suffering God.

But how do you come to this judgement about your God? You have chosen your God.

No, I have not chosen my God. God has chosen the kind of experience, if you like that word, which he gave me. It is not my choice; it is a kind of revelation which God has made to me of Himself.

But you do choose. You go to the experts, you say, who have the experience. But there are many people who would give you different advice, who still claim to have had direct, genuine experience.

I am always ready to listen to them.

And then you discern for yourself what is valuable and what is not.

I think it is God who is guiding me in my interpretation and choice.

"God" then seems to be just a name for what you think is the most valuable reality.

I am entirely for the elimination of the word "God". The word does not mean anything. It conveys nothing precise or informative or illuminating about Him.

It's in the Bible, unlike "religion" and "mysticism".

It's not in the Bible. In the Bible He has a very personal name, Jahweh. The Old Testament never talks of God in the abstract. I think we have evacuated the word "God" of any meaning. In reality if we wanted our prayer to be genuine we should in each case address God personally in connection with the present need that makes us pray to Him at that moment. There are moments when I should say to Him, "Lord of Beauty"; other moments when I should say "Lord of Truth". Not "God", which is simply an abstraction.

Where do you get the notion of unity, behind these different aspects of God?

I think that all these qualifications we give to God, all our applications to God for some need, can always be reduced to something which is a declaration we receive from God: "thou art beloved": the very words addressed by the angel to the prophet Daniel. And my reaction, "I love Thee, and I love others" — it is the gospel. "What shall I do to have eternal life?" says the gospel; and "Thou shalt love the Lord thy God with all thy heart, with thy whole self." That's all.

But this did not mean that you should love whatever, in the widest sense, has a meaning for you.

I think that a very important word in that sentence of Jesus is *"thy"*. "The Lord thy God" is a God whom you can experience as *thy* God.

Could you say something about evil?

For me the problem of evil is insoluble if you separate it from the idea of a fall. The real tragedy did not happen with the first man but with the first separation of what the gospel calls the power of darkness, the Prince of Darkness. There was at a certain moment a clash which we cannot know about fully, a separation. Since then, creatures who were made to synchronize, to co-operate, began to be perverted by developing themselves independently. I agree with Teilhard de Chardin when he says that the origin of evil may be found already in biology when a tissue or a cell wants to live an independent life, not depending any more on the others. Then you have cancer beginning. Cancer is really a model of evil because it is a type of something which declares itself independent and wants to grow independently, breaking the co-operation with other elements. There was a certain time, a time of refusal, when God asked a "yes" or "no" from certain powers. And some said "no", and in saying "no" they became independent. And the whole harmony of the universe was shattered. Then different biological species began to eat each other, the struggle for existence began, and so on. That is not what God wanted.

Now I think that God is a suffering God, not sitting on a throne but struggling with us, among us. And during the struggle it happens to Him to be wounded, even to be killed apparently in such and such souls. And yet we believe that He is stronger in the end. How could a God who is all-powerful, as I believe, yet at the same time be a suffering God? To be a suffering God does not mean that suffering may be forced upon him. God cannot be forced into anything. But he can voluntarily, spontaneously, assume human suffering in himself — sharing in our suffering because it is necessary in order that our own "yes" to him may be quite free.

He wants us to say "yes" to Him. If we are to say "yes" with any validity we must be able to say "no". And if we are able to say "no", that opens the door to all the denial, refusal, unhappiness, catastrophes and so on.

I wonder how far this idea of a once existing harmony which has now been broken is, in your view, related to the experience which many people record of a kind of "oceanic" feeling, a sense of cosmic unity, of being in some way one with their surroundings — the sort of thing Wordsworth described?

I think that already in this life this harmony, this unity, may be established by some privileged people. I think there are people, saints for instance, who may acquire a power over the physical world, the animal and vegetable world.

But this establishment of an actual harmony is perhaps something different from the momentary vision which many people describe having.

Well, this moment of vision is part and parcel of the original harmony, I think; an anticipation of what we shall have, of what we may have.

What of the Christian doctrine of the creation, that it is very good?

It *was* very good. I think what is very important is what has happened in the world of angels. I firmly believe in a world of angels that is more important than our human world. I think great decisions have been taken in the world of angels — and of devils.

I think that the only decent presentation of the great person of the devil is the Moslem one. The Christian presentation is a caricature. The Moslem Satan is Iblis. The sin of Iblis was an excess of love for God. He was so enticed by the beauty of God, the splendour of God, that he could not bear the idea that God might one day come among men. He rejected the idea in order to safeguard the uniqueness of God, the supreme beauty of God. That is the Moslem conception, which is very beautiful.

But isn't it the element of independence that you felt to be central to the Christian conception of the fall?

I think the link between the two conceptions is a certain search for nobility and purity. Satan is not to be looked for in the caricature conceptions of the western world. He is a person of great nobility, beauty and greatness. He remains a Prince of the angels. And the real temptations coming from Satan are not low temptations, like those of the instincts. They come in the most beautiful forms of the intellectual, the moral, the spiritual and the aesthetic: developments separate from God. They are in every artistic creation that leads us to despair, or which is an expression of despair. And now I shall say something which may scandalize you. I consider the works of Wagner, and music such as the ninth symphony of Beethoven, and Chopin's Nocturnes, as diabolically influenced, because they often express sheer despair, without any ray of hope for the eternal world. If you want to look for Satan, look in sublime works; in what is extremely beautiful, great but separated.

But do these not express genuine experience?

Yes, but there is no place left for God in them.

But is not God found in the existential awareness of despair, and in facing up to this?

Yes, if this despair is transformed by a ray of light, God would be there. But if it is as in Schopenhauer, for instance, that is diabolical.

But despair can in fact be a creative state. Many people describe how they have only been able to reach a new awareness of truth as a result of total despair; they feel themselves at the very bottom.

Then you come back to this image which I spoke of, when I experienced myself as lying flat on the earth and being unable to go further down. Like a ball which hits the ground, and must then bounce back. But there are people who remain down, and do not see a ray of light.

Could I come back to Bergson? How would you interpret his idea of the élan *vital in religious terms? What relation has this to what we should call religious experience?*

Jung has made a link between them. For him the libido was the *élan* vital. There is a tendency towards something ever greater, reaching, as Teilhard de Chardin would say, towards the Omega Point.

But is the élan *vital something immanent, or is it something that comes from beyond man?*

From beyond man, yes. Bergson wrote specifically in a sentence I remember: "I believe in a God, free and personal, free and a creator."

But Jung's idea of libido is not as transcendent as that.

In the last two years of his life Jung thought of this *élan* as really existing. And to this he added his idea of the Archetypes, from the beginning still acting upon us.

Do you believe that evil may take an initiative? When we talk of guidance, I think of demons disguised as angels of light.

There are very definite criteria to judge guidance. First of all a guidance should not come only once; it must be repeated. Secondly, it must be spoken with the style of God; that is very important. God has his own language, his own style. Grammatically I should say you can recognize a sentence spoken by God. Thirdly, you may test a guidance by sharing this guidance with other people. Ask four or five people who understand your problem to pray for a solution and to ask for guidance, and see whether the answers are convergent. Fourthly, the most definitive: does this guidance create in you sorrow, bitterness, hatred? Or does it create in you joy and love for God and other people? Judge the tree according to the fruit.

Could you say something about the style? Different people describe it in different ways. The varieties of religious experience reflect the varieties of God's grammar. How can you say, this is the true style, this is false? And what if someone disagrees with you about this style?

I have asked such questions of several people, and I found that they agreed on the style of God. But often in their interpretation, their development of the words spoken by God they tried to formulate them humanly — in long sentences which cannot be attributed to God. God speaks always in very short sentences, very short. He does not generally go further than five or six words. They are spoken in a way for which I can only find one adjective, FINAL. He doesn't leave the door open to any argument, contestation, or question. I think these are the two characteristics, great brevity and the absoluteness of it.

Many people who write to us say that their first awareness of this other dimension came in the form of doubts. Questions began to raise themselves. This seems to be a different matter from the final, authoritative, definitive pronouncement. It is rather a sense of incomprehension.

Then it is another matter. It is what I should call the method of infiltration by God. You will remember the episode in the gospel of the two disciples on the road to Emmaus. They are discussing between themselves, when Jesus comes up. Generally in the gospel when He meets people He is facing them. This is the only case in which He approaches them from behind. He follows them, listens to them, and hears them, and enters into their talk. This is not the way of speaking with authority but the method of infiltration. He can enter us as ink can penetrate blotting paper.

There may then be those who are aware of no guidance at the time, nothing transcendent, but later they will look back and see a pattern; they will see that doors were opened and closed.

Yes, that happens.

I wonder if you are interested in the ideas of Michael Polanyi, when he distinguishes between explicit and tacit knowledge, and suggests that tacit knowledge is more fundamental than explicit knowledge. I think that explicit knowledge has added to tacit knowledge in a continuous process.

I am only anxious not to mix what is science with what is not science, that is to say, what is not verifiable, not measurable.

But not all science can be reduced to terms of material things.

I don't reduce reality to material things. I am now speaking only of the criteria of scientific knowledge.

Would Bergson have admitted that the élan *vital was open to scientific investigation?*

No. He insisted on this point.

Then how is his philosophy to be defended against the charge of producing a deus ex machina in this élan *vital, a sort of God of the gaps to fit into the parts that science can't explain?*

For Bergson it was simple: he relied not on science but on intuition, and intuition was something entirely different from a scientific approach.

And the critic would say that this nicely removes the problem into a realm where you cannot question it. According to Polanyi there is no need to take this sort of defensive action, since in his view science is more dependent on intuition than it is at present ready to recognize.

Let us not complicate things. I am speaking of scientific *knowledge.* When I say that King Louis XVIth was beheaded on the 21st January 1793, I speak of something that is verifiable. That is scientific knowledge. But there is much that is not scientific *knowledge.* We speak about the laws of nature: there are no such things. We have only the calculus of probabilities and statistics. For instance you cannot prove that there cannot be a resurrection of the dead. The only thing we can say is that up till now we have had no scientifically verifiable case of the resurrection of a dead man. It doesn't mean that because 99 have not risen again the 100th will not rise again. It's a question of probability: there are no laws. Laws of nature are a fiction of the imagination. For myself I see no conflict between religion and science because they never mix in any way.

Then we live in a dualistic order?

Exactly, I agree with you. From the point of view of knowledge we can never mix what is verifiable and what is not. We live in a dualistic world from the point of view of knowledge. But I don't say that scientific knowledge gives us the *essence* of the world.

3

Martin Israel

One of the questions we are most frequently asked is this: "What kind of experience counts as religious? What exactly is *a religious experience?" It is a question we have not yet ourselves given a definite answer to. But in the end I am sure we shall have to.*

I would say that religious experience is an experience of that which transcends the individual and makes him a fuller individual, which makes the personality more integrated in terms of understanding his place in the world; an experience that there is something outside him, of which he has been made aware, that broadens his view of life, something that gives him a widened awareness, and brings him to thoughts of deity. It comes spontaneously; it is not intellectually induced. This could include aspects of psychic experience. I am sure there is a difference between religious and ordinary psychic experience, but I don't think it would be wise to draw an artificial dividing line. The religious includes the psychical, but the psychical does not necessarily include the religious. All experiences from simple telepathy up to the greatest mystical experience are psychical experiences; but a telepathic experience or a clairvoyant one doesn't necessarily involve a religious or mystical dimension. There is such a spectrum of psychical experience that it is probably better to take the lot and divide them into your own categories in due course, rather than reject any at once.

Yes, this is just what we have been doing. We tend to disregard cases which are simply telepathic, with no religious significance at all. I mean cases when a person writes saying, "I thought of Mr. A., and at that moment he rang me up on the telephone." That was all. I don't call that a religious experience. But, as you were saying, I think that many of these experiences are related to the religious; and I agree that there is a sense in which all religious experience can be described as psychical.

By psychical I mean mediated by modes of perception outside the five senses, or coming from a source that cannot be detected by the five senses. It may be manifested by one's hearing something or seeing something, but there is no object within the ordinary sense of the word which causes the perception.

One of the questions which is often raised is how far religious experience is culturally determined. Some people would say that all such experience is purely a product of environment, upbringing, culture, and so forth. How can one counter this argument?

The only way you can counter it is by investigating the cultural environment of the individual. I had a remarkable religious experience at the age of sixteen, which involved out-of-the-body experience, and being shown the transcendence of God, and the fact of rebirth. And I came from a background that knew nothing of these things at all, so much so that I kept this experience away from my family (and everybody) for many years. So I know that my personal experience was something spontaneous, and not related to anything that I had come in contact with in my background. I can't say that I had never read anything about this sort of thing, because one can't vouch for everything one had read before the age of sixteen, but it was so new to me from this level that it made a great impression on me. Before that I had had psychical experience, so as to be aware of other modalities of existence, but again in an environment that was materialistic and extremely hostile to this way of thought. You undoubtedly must investigate the cultural and religious background of your subject to see if there is a correlation; this could be extremely valuable.

We can only follow up a limited number of cases of course; we shall have to select.

Yes. The most promising ones are those that are generally ignorant about these matters. Those who are highly knowledgeable are, on the one hand, more liable to talk themselves into believing they have had experiences, yet, on the other hand, their intellectual attitude may make them less receptive to the very experiences they are interested in. If they come from a background in which these experiences are regarded as peculiar or alien, then their testimony of an experience is particularly important. Of course people from an "esoteric" background can also have genuine spiritual experiences, but these must be analysed with particular care.

Martin Israel

A lot of people describe episodes from their childhood, and say how at the time they seemed to be "ineffable" or "indescribable" or something quite unrelated to their previous experience. This seems to give some support to the idea that there can be experiences of this kind for which a person's culture has provided no words for him to describe them.

This is true. They come as a bolt from the blue, even to those who come from a traditional religious background. And they have a glory, as it were, that seems to come from outside that traditional religious background, so that traditional religion does not live up to them, to these experiences of what it seems we always knew in our very being.

Could I return for a moment to the question of telepathy? Even a single telepathic experience may sometimes have a significant effect on a person's life, though at the time it may be thought of as nothing more than a remarkable coincidence.

I would agree that such an experience may at first seem nothing more to a person than an interesting oddity. But, if on the other hand, as you are postulating, this experience has had a life-transforming effect then it is more than just that; it is also a spiritual experience.

Yes, in itself it may not bring about a sudden transformation; it may only contain a germ, leading to a later progression.

It may indeed, and this is why we should never discount psychical experience. My feeling is that all experiences should be collected, and then they can be put into categories. Some may indeed turn out to be trivial; others of a rather similar type may be found to be very important. We can't judge, except by the life of the person.

What you are saying is that one cannot tell whether an experience is religious until it has, so to speak, taken root.

Yes.

Many people would say that telepathic experience is simply a psychical phenomenon; they would give no spiritual interpretation to it at all. They may regard telepathy as something like radiation. I wouldn't call that a religious experience.

If you are wanting a religious experience primarily you should say it should be marked by a sudden accession of some type of knowledge or power that heightens the life of the individual and makes him more aware of the nature or reality; that brings him to an encounter with deity.

There is no reason why an experience which subsequently turns out to be illusory may not at the time have a life-transforming effect.

It is indeed possible to have such an experience, both on a level of personal relationships in which one misinterprets the attitude of another individual, and on the psychical level, in which one mistakes telepathy or precognition for the sudden remembrance of a detail long stored up in the unconscious mind and brought to light by a particular encounter in real life. But a truly spiritual experience transcends purely personal details and satisfaction, and brings the person into fellowship with so vast a dimension of life and love that his whole understanding of reality is revolutionised.

Isn't it possible to have an experience which is in some way transpersonal and life-transforming which is not at the same time life-enhancing, analogous to a psychotic breakdown or depression or something of this sort, but which is also religious?

Yes, this type of experience can occur as part of the disintegration of the personality that takes place in some psychotic episodes. But of even greater importance is the apparently genuine life-enhancing experience with strongly mystical overtones that may occur in other types of psychosis, especially those associated with recurrent manic-depressive episodes. While many workers in the field would dismiss these simply as aspects of disturbed mental function, it is possible that they could be a genuine opening of consciousness to higher aspects of reality in a person whose normal intellectual balance was disturbed. It is even possible that such an experience could form a central focus around which a healed personality could form when the disease process was brought under control. The eighteenth-century poet, Christopher Smart, was such a psychotic, who could nevertheless bring forth remarkable poetry with high religious insight during periods of ecstasy.

Some of the experiences which we have put on one side as coming from the mentally disturbed may well be very important from a psychiatric point of view.

This could be an important subsidiary contribution of the study of religious experience.

Martin Israel

I should like to go back for a moment to what you were saying about illusion. It wouldn't worry me if one felt intellectually that a great deal of the spread of Christianity was based on an illusion to begin with. it would not alter the validity of the message of the gospel or of the whole spirit of it. I mean, there was a delusion at that time that the world was coming to an end, and that many people then living would not die. That gave a unique atmosphere at the time. We know that that was wrong. And it could be that the appearances of Christ were of the nature of apparitions to the people who had known him, just as happened to Wilfred Owen's brother. He had this strong apparition just at the time of his brother's death — we don't know what really happened. But just as under hypnosis a strong impression of a person may be given, it may be that it was an illusion. Something like that I believe is true of the appearances of Christ. But they gave a great boost to early Christianity; they gave it its force; they rallied all the people who had scattered after the crucifixion. Even if they were shown to have been an illusion it wouldn't worry me. The message of the gospel, of the loving father, of this relationship to something beyond the self — this is the important thing. I'm not bothered by things like the resurrection at all.

I appreciate this point of view, and many modernistic Christians would admit to doubting the literal resurrection of Jesus and yet still affirm the Christian faith. But how much stronger that faith would be if the paranormal events described in the gospel were literally true and not figments of the fertile imaginations of the disciples! Mormonism is an example of a modern religious cult that arose around the private revelations of its prophet Joseph Smith. While few outside the circle of this sect could respond positively to these revelations, it cannot be denied that Mormonism fills the spiritual needs of a considerable number of people, especially in the United States.

How far do you think one should encourage curiosity about psychic levels of experience, particularly among younger people? If in religious education the whole approach of dogmatic Christianity seems dead, may it be that curiosity about psychical experience may be a sort of way in to an appreciation of levels of spirituality which are otherwise inaccessible?

I am sure that the modern generation will accept truth only through the medium of experience and experiment. Dogma in itself is essential to all teaching but it cannot be impressed on intelligent people from outside. It has to grow from within the person. It is certain that we are going to see much more experimentation in states of consciousness in the future, and it is important that there should be experts available who know about psychic as well as mystical aspects of reality. Prejudice against the psychic mode is unhelpful, because many people are psychically gifted as a natural endowment.

I used to be concerned with the training of students who were going out to teach religious education, and the idea that they should be equipped with knowledge of psychical experience in order to cope with this kind of curiosity — this idea would never have occurred to them at all.

This is one of the great differences that has taken place in the religious scene in recent years. But remember that the psychic is only a gateway to the deeper spiritual reality that underlies all existence. To get stuck on the psychic level is as sad a state of affairs to be immersed in as secular humanism.

Would it be possible for you to say in a few sentences what the importance of the Christ is for you?

To me Christ is the Uncreated Word of God deeply implanted in the soul of all people (the light that lighteth every man), who has been with God before creation. I believe this Word has been deeply eloquent in the lives of many great saints and mystics, but that in the one whom Christians call the Christ — Jesus of Nazareth — the Word is perfectly shown in human form, so that the human can be the vehicle of deity. Through participating in the life that was in Jesus, humanity can attain release from bondage to the selfishness of sin and enter a new relationship with God of which love for the neighbour, who is every fellow human being — and ultimately every form of life — is the outer manifestation.

There is much talk these days of the "New Age", expressed in various ways such as a coming "change in vibrations" or other apocalyptic events. Is this, do you think, a reflection in some people's minds of some kind of cosmic dissatisfaction or unrest?

Yes, I do believe, there is a cosmic dissatisfaction in the minds of some people, especially the younger generation. Humanistic secularism has a limited appeal to the aspirations of people, and the mainstream religions seem to be earth-bound, either in social good works or in incomprehensible dogma, to a great many people. Esoteric studies cater for the worst of this type of person, while at the same time taking him away from the pressing responsibilities of his everyday world. Admittedly some "New Age" folk are spiritually advanced, but most of the ones I have met have obvious personality inadequacies that prevent them relating properly to their fellows in everyday life. True spirituality consists in doing the next piece of work ahead of one as perfectly as possible — to the greater glory of God, one might say.

There is quite an eschatological feeling about some of this talk about changes of vibrations and so on.

People were expecting the world to come to an end two thousand years ago, and this played an important part in the early Christian teaching. It could be that something like this is in the wind now, but it is scarcely new.

Perhaps it is linked up with the idea of an atomic chain-reaction.

Yes, I would agree that mankind's harnessing of nuclear energy and the possible abuse of this source of power does bring the idea of the end of the world into more urgent perspective.

Psychic energy can generate physical energy, surely.

It may well be that there is an important connection, but we cannot define it at present. There are great difficulties of terminology here, and one really should not use the same word "energy" if it implies that there is some common element which is in any way transferable from one field to another. Where so many people have gone wrong, like, for instance, some radionics practitioners, is in the assumption that there is a ready conversion factor between the psychical and the physical. This is in fact without any foundation.

You spoke earlier of a mystical awareness of us being all one, and of the unity of all things mental and physical. Do you think one can draw a distinct boundary round the individual personality or soul?

Heraclitus said, you cannot define the boundaries of the soul, so deep are they. And yet paradoxically enough there is an individual identity for each one of us. In a way the Christian idea of the Trinity is of help here. I am intimately involved with you when I communicate with you, which I should do always if I were in proper communion with you. Pure communication is absolute. And yet you and I can never be the same; we have our own identities. But the more I am in communion with you, the more does my own identity expand. The more I am in community, the more all-embracing is my own identity. The more separate I am, the smaller is my range.

The whole concept of individuality is a most difficult one in biology. When you look at a film showing for example the speeded up movements of phagocytes, cells in our own body, sometimes acting as individuals, sometimes moving about like packs of wolves destroying things, one may perhaps feel that our individual consciousness is somehow in the sum of the individual consciousnesses of all the cells in our body. J. B. S. Haldane in his book The Uniqueness of Man *conceives of the idea of the deity as a great mind: just as the cells of our body make up our consciousness, so do all the consciousnesses of humanity make up a much greater one. It is arguable that our idea of transcendence may come from our individual relationship with this larger thing outside. We don't know how big it is.*

I think this is too superficial a view. This individual relationship that you speak of brings us into mystical union with the totality of being. Transcendence and immanence join to form one stream as we become aware of the all in ALL.

In your work of spiritual healing what sort of guide-lines do you keep in mind?

The guide-line that I try to keep in mind is that the person may reach the fulness of the measure of the stature of Christ; in other words that he may be guided to see the true nature of reality. True healing is not merely the healing of the body, although this is vital; it is the healing of the whole personality, which is a triad of body, mind and spirit, the soul being the highest part of the mind, and the spirit being something which is both of us and not of us: that of God in every man.

There are healers that don't seem to be concerned with any spiritual aspect. Are they healing only a psychic level?

Yes, the great majority of so-called spiritual healers work on the psychic level. This is no condemnation; some of them do good work. As I have said before, we cannot correlate psychical effects by means of physical measurement. Many of these healers have elaborate theories involving energies, frequencies and so on, which alienate the scientist, so that there is no real communication. Such healing is a very capricious business: sometimes it works and sometimes it doesn't. It often occurs when you least expect it, and vice versa. That is why this is only a small part of the healing process: it can work in collaboration with other agencies of healing but cannot supplant them.

There is this paradox, isn't there, that healing is right and yet at the same time suffering can be transforming.

Yes, but suffering would be irrelevant if there were not the hope of healing. Unrelieved suffering is indeed diabolical. Suffering becomes redeeming only when you are given the vision of the continuity of life. If you were sure that this was the only life, and you were in hell now, there would be no possibility of a sense of purpose or of God. Suffering can transform; very often it doesn't. In the totality of existence one can hope to see the light; in one life it is very difficult, if not impossible. Didn't Job's wife advise "curse God and die"? The majority of people would take the same view.

Would you agree that we cannot really use spiritual healing as a separate technique, but only as part of a larger process involving a complete understanding of what God's will is for us?

Yes, I would say that spiritual healing can never really be successful until people are more spiritually-minded. Until we move nearer to one another in love we cannot hope that more will be revealed. And this may apply to psychical phenomena as well. To me ESP is essentially a matter of deep communication one with another. We know that the closer two people are together emotionally in the more likely they are to telepathize. As one advances in relationship one is better able to communicate. And under these conditions these other things are added to you, both ESP and mystical experience. People who really love each other are never separated even by death. There are not many people who really know such a relationship. As we give ourselves in relationship, so many of these things begin to come to us, and then we may become fit instruments to transmit them. I think that the psychical will ultimately be explained scientifically, because I believe that science is the measure of all things in the universe. But it will be a new sort of science, not the science we have today.

Do you believe that science will be able ultimately to penetrate all the mysteries of the universe? Or that there will ever come a time when there are no mysteries left to be explored?

I believe that there is no final mystery in the creation itself; the mystery lies in the creator. In other words I believe that all creation is governed by law. There is a law of relationships as well. The law of synchronicity that Jung speaks about is, I believe, a law of relationships, of how things work together. And I feel that as we come to know ourselves more in the true Christ-like way, so more will be revealed to us. After all the end of knowledge is to cast out fear. That is the law of love. If the scientific way is right, it shows us how God works in the world. Everything is susceptible to law; there is a law of our own being, and as we grow in stature we shall penetrate that mystery also. Whether we can every know everything is a pointless question. All we can say is that we shall know more and more about things that are mysterious today when we ourselves have grown in spiritual stature. And perhaps it is not such a bad thing that we do not at present know much about psychic phenomena; what a terrible thing it would be, for example, if people were able to transmit propaganda telepathically.

When you have a mystical experience, does this come directly from the creator? Or is it through some sort of law in the universe that this higher illumination comes?

Everything proceeds from the Creator, who is beyond conception and definition, but in some way comes to the creature in a personal mode. I believe a true mystical experience is a direct apprehension of God the Creator by the human soul, by an act of love on the part of the Creator. Whether celestial hierarchies (the Communion of Saints) are also involved I do not know, but I think it very probable that they are.

Yes, I think one can only approach God as if he were a person.

There is something in the nature of the heart of reality which cares infinitely for each created thing. This is the great religious postulate. Not only us but the smallest organism, the most minute crystal, everything that has form. This you can never transmit to another person. To one who is suffering it seems that his pain can't possibly justify such a postulate. That's where faith really does come in. You can't give it to another person; you can only live it yourself.

I'm a terrible heretic biologically, and when I look down a microscope and see in a drop of pond-water life like Piccadilly Circus I find I cannot deny the possibility of consciousness even to the lowest forms of life, indeed throughout the whole creation. I can't see where you draw any line.

I think that what we call life implies soul of some kind. Of course you can't prove that there is consciousness in what we call the inanimate, but I expect this too is right basically.

Would you say that you were a Taoist?

Yes, definitely. I think that view of reality is very helpful. There is a balance in all things, an order in everything.

4

Rosalind Heywood

One of the difficulties we're up against in this field is the variety of ways in which different people use words like "natural" and "supernatural", "normal" and "paranormal". Our starting point is basically that the religious is a quite natural element in human experience; but other people take a rather different view.

To my mind this is a matter of semantics about which I can't pretend to know anything. But if I'm convinced of anything it is that the universe is one, and I don't see how you can have one bit of the universe "normal" and the other bit "paranormal" in any real sense. Unless you simply mean by the word paranormal something which we haven't yet discovered.

Would you say there are certain gifts, aptitudes, faculties and so forth which do not occur normally in the human race, or would you say that they are universal but neglected or suppressed?

I take it you mean things that are labelled ESP? I don't care for the word. But is that what you mean?

Yes, when people say they have "the sight" or that sort of thing.

Let me say what I *feel*, rather than what I *think*. I feel that at some subliminal level we are all interlinked — as, so we are told, are the so-called basic particles of matter. I suspect that the problem lies in bringing subliminal reactions to some unknown kind of impression up to consciousness. The material may get distorted on the way up, or, I suspect, very often, and in some people more than others, it may never reach surface consciousness at all. I cannot give you any reason why I feel that, subliminally, all human beings — all living creatures — are interlinked. But I had fifty-six years experience of telepathic interaction surfacing between my husband and myself, mostly when it served a useful purpose. Such frequency may have been because we were very fond of each other, but I don't see why it should be confined to people with such close links, even if it occurs more frequently between them.

This telepathic interaction can be tiresome. A few years ago, two days after my husband had flown to South Africa, I happened to smash my hip-bone. I was terribly worried. I thought, "If I write and tell him he'll probably rush back and then there will be nobody to cook for him. And if I die it will probably be before he gets back. I do want him to stay in South Africa where I know he will be properly looked after until I can manage." But I also thought, "If I don't tell him, he'll probably pick up that I've been pretty badly knocked around." Finally I forbade my sons to tell him till it was clear I was going to survive. But I got a frantic letter, written *before* he could *normally* have expected to hear from me, saying, "I'm extremely worried about you. Why haven't you written? I don't know what is the matter." And he made a great fuss to his family in Durban that something was wrong with me. Well, that was my problem. If I had let him know at once he would have come home, to his discomfort and my worry. If I didn't, he would pick up that I was in trouble, and worry himself.

Yes, this is where there is some link between two minds. Something surely different applies where a mind seems to pick up things which are not in somebody else's mind: clairvoyance or something like that?

Personally, I feel so utterly ignorant of the whole process of ESP in general that I can only repeat that I feel that every living creature is interlinked with every other — and if so, why shouldn't the interlinkage go further? Matter is only a form of energy. A magnet attracts or repels another magnet. I find it hard to envisage, but I don't see why there should not be interaction with something that is not in someone else's mind. We know so little — so very little . . .

I have a prejudice about the idea of clairvoyance when it just means knowing what's on the other side of a card which has never been seen by any visual or sensory system.

So have I. But my betters tell me *that* it happens, so I think, "Well, one day you'll learn *how* it happens!"

The statistics, I'm sure, suggest that there are people who are good at guessing what's on the other side of a card. But I think that's different from the kind of clairvoyance where one holds an object which is closely associated with a person. Psychometry involves a personality and I feel it's something rather different.

Yes, that idea seems easier to take. I've even done it myself. The object seems to provide a link. But I loathe it when somebody gives me a pack of cards to guess through. I want to throw it at them.

Do you think an ability of this kind which one may label psychic may be driven out of one, or at least suppressed or discouraged, by certain kinds of education?

I would guess so — an education which emphasizes the analytical approach. But is it also possible — again I speak with great diffidence — that when children get older they are so busy dealing with this aspect of the world as presented by the senses that it takes up all their time and attention? When my elder son was just six I showed him a book of pictures from the National Gallery and he said, "Oh, a mummy and child", or "a cart", "a tree" and so on. I then, in just the same way, showed him one of the less intelligible Picasso paintings and he looked at me rather pityingly and tapped his forehead and said, "Oh, that goes on *inside* your head, not outside". But I showed him some Picassos again when he was twelve and he said, "Oh, I don't know what to make of that lot." It seemed to me that another part of him, so to speak, had become uppermost.

Looking back on your own life, do you think that something like this happened to you yourself?

I think that even as a child I experienced what I can only call *imageless* ESP. For instance I was terrified of a "presence" I couldn't see in a bedroom where I was put to sleep and where, so my mother told me after I was grown up, she and her sister had seen an apparition. But of course such things were never mentioned to children! I lived in a world where they talked about cricket, not psychology. And of course I didn't say anything either. I was frightened of ghosts until, after I was grown-up, I saw one; and one didn't talk about one's fears, as a child I mean. Nobody said anything about anything. But I now think that I was aware of what people were like "inside". So, I expect, are many children.

I think what may have been ESP began to function actively when I went as an under-age V.A.D. in the first World War. Then there were good reasons for it. One would be responsible for dangerously sick patients and yet not able to get at a doctor or a trained nurse. Then something said, "Do this" or "Do that". That was in connection with healing. The ESP was *needed.* It was also needed in connection with my marriage. My husband was always a very reserved, uncommunicative person on the surface and I think that may have enabled more communication to go on between us beneath the surface, because we loved each other. An inner "to and fro" went on between us all our lives, and I think that may have stimulated my mild capacity for ESP in relation to other people too. Then I met a few people who told me about investigation into ESP and gave me books to read. It seemed to me vitally important. Next Mrs. Alfred Lyttelton took me into the Society for Psychical Research and I found a whole new world there. And I realised that my parlour game of hand reading at diplomatic dinner-parties had taught me things about people that nobody had told me.

About this hand reading, some people would say that the information one gets from it, or a crystal ball, or even a tea-cup, is basically within oneself, and the external visible thing one is looking at is only activating something which is already potentially part of one's knowledge.

This is one of those either/or questions which always unnerve me. As for hand reading — well, obviously we all know that a good square solid hand indicates a person who differs from one with a little thin hand. But I have also learnt from experience, absurd though it sounds, that the size, depth and relationships of various lines *can* tell one something about a person. I mean, you can judge the information they give you intellectually. But, as you say, on the other hand, to concentrate on a hand, or a crystal, or bones, or entrails, or tea-leaves, or anything for that matter, occupies — stills — the conscious mind. It ceases to bash around, so to speak, and that seems to give information from beyond consciousness a chance to seep up to the surface. In a book, *The Art of Scientific Investigation*, Professor W. I. B. Beveridge shows how often creative ideas come to the surface when the conscious mind is gently occupied. It needs to be quietly ticking over. Or you may go to sleep and dream. The point is to keep the conscious mind from interfering, from analysing.

You said a moment ago in connection with your nursing that somebody told you this or something told you that. What do you imply by that — a sort of impulse?

I wish I knew. It's almost impossible to describe, any more than you can describe what you mean when you look at a daffodil and *know* that it is beautiful. I can't say that some outside personality told me things and I can't say that I just acted on impulse. If I say "command" it's wrong. It may be another level of one's own psyche which has wider vision than one's conscious little ego. I don't know what it is. When you want to help, it just says, "Do that".

It gave you good advice.

I've never known it give me bad advice. Not when it comes in that authoritative way. Obviously one has mistaken impulses. That's different. Occasionally it seems to come from some discarnate person, in connection with someone they have loved on earth. That may be so, but I can't be sure as I'm not sure that there are discarnate persons. But I behave as if they were genuine, and then it feels as if there were a source which I can recognise as exterior to myself. But sometimes I have no sense of a source.

I was talking not long ago with a lady in the North of Scotland who was not conventionally religious but said that as long as she could remember she always had the ability when she was in a tight corner of what she called "plugging in" to some kind of source of external power; and of getting not so much an answer as a reassurance from it that everything in fact was going to be all right. She said she could do this any time — when she was on top of a bus, or in the bath. This was distinctly an intiative on her part, and not just a hoping that something would tap her on the shoulder and say it was going to be all right. How would you comment on this?

I accept it absolutely, but I lack it myself. I never seem to have any of this sort of experience unless it's to do with other people or with — I think the only word I can use is beauty. It may be beauty on a mountain, or on the sea, in a cathedral or where you will. Beauty will get me out of myself; it's as if beauty were one of the absolutes. It's difficult to put into words but I think that it makes you entirely forget your little ego, which seems to me the first step towards real awareness of anything else. This is possibly why in nursing, when you didn't know anything, you had so entirely forgotten your ego that instructions were, so to speak, able to come through.

Rosalind Heywood

Do you think that lack of normal communication facilitates telepathy? The only one of our children I have really noticed it with is the youngest. The only times when he seems to me to do it and be right is when I'm abstracted from him and brooding, or thinking about something, and he will suddenly say something like "I wonder if Granny has a new dog", just when I'm thinking about my mother.

Those to me would be ideal conditions — where he really needed communication, and you are "brooding".

I sometimes find in a group that it's often the person who isn't communicating who interests one and draws one out. And just occasionally one feels that one does know more about them in some mysterious way than the other people who have been talking.

Yes, with some people one feels in tune — there's some resonance, and with others there isn't — however hard you try there just isn't. Two notes that are out of tune are out of tune.

We have a letter from someone who practices what he calls "the prayer of visualisation". When he wants to pray for somebody he forms in his own mind a picture of them, he creates a little scene, and in it he hears the nurse saying "Your temperature is down now, you may go home tomorrow". And he does this every morning and it eventually works. He goes along and the girl says, "You know what the nurse said to me? 'Your temperature is down now, you may go home tomorrow'." And he has a number of cases like this. Where he feels God comes into it I'm not sure. Isn't this analogous to sympathetic magic?

Yes, maybe. Perhaps sympathetic magic is another word for that. But actually you've reminded me of an old man, Dr. Hector Monroe. He was a Celtic doctor who had Lister's rooms just off Regents Park. He was extremely gifted with ESP and he told me once that he had an old, very rich, very grand, very difficult, very self-willed patient and nothing would do her any good. She was supposed to go to see him the next day. That night he decided to go to bed and picture her well, younger and happy. The next morning her nurse rang up and asked if she should wake her because she was in the first really good sleep she had had for ages. So he decided that that was one way of doctoring.

There's a question I would like to ask you all very much, and that's on the subject of visual imagery. I had a great friend, a naval inventor called Vivian Usborne. He knew he was going to die: he had leukemia.

I used to go and see him, and he was convinced, and I was too at that time, that at death you snuffed out. He complained to me bitterly that all the inventions which were still simmering in his brain would never come to fruition. I was afraid so too. To cut a rather elaborate story short, about 10 days after his death I appeared to run into him, absolutely slap, like you run into somebody in the street. It was indoors. So I stood still and closed my eyes so as not to lose contact and Vivian appeared to say, "We were quite wrong; I've got scope and opportunity beyond my wildest dreams". This seemed perfectly normal. So I said (and "said" is a very remote word), "This is absolutely marvellous, Vivian", and I felt, so to speak, caught up into this scope and opportunity. And then I suddenly remembered my duty and said, "This is all very well but you haven't given me any evidence. What about the S.P.R.?" Vivian said, "I can't give you any evidence because you have no *concepts* for these conditions. I can only give you poetic *images."* He then gave me a very good image. I held on as long as I could, then I had to say, "I'm sorry, I can't hold on any longer, I must drop now."

It was only gradually borne in on me, largely through talking to Sir Cyril Burt, who told me about visualisers and audiles, how much our awareness of finer realms of being — I'm trying to use very general terms — has to be translated into the kind of images which we use in our cultural and conscious three-dimensional world. You will find some mediums talking of green fields and other mediums talking of celestial music. I found a report the other day of two educated women who were staying with a Bishop. They were in a room together and one thought she saw a kind of celestial figure, and said so, and the other said she heard celestial music. They both used the word "celestial". Well, was one a visualiser and one an audile?

In the descriptions of religious experiences you receive, are you getting images made from our kind of existence of things of which the writers have no concepts, but which they have translated into images according to their own temperaments?

What was the image your friend gave you?

It sounds banal but it was perfect. It was a swan with tremendous wings flying very very high in a limitless blue sky. For unlimited scope and opportunity it couldn't have been better, although it sounds a bit Victorian. The experience of being told that I had no concepts, that I must be given an image, and then getting it — thwack! — was very impressive to me.

Was this without words?

It depends what you mean by words. Words spoken by that mouth here and this mouth here are a very remote affair compared with, I was almost going to say, "direct communication". Whether it was in the form of words, or just ideas, or whether you can have an idea without the words, I can't tell you. I certainly didn't have to wait a long time while that was said. It was immediate. You know that story of Mozart being aware of a whole symphony in a moment, simultaneously, so to speak, and afterwards writing it down sequentially. I sometimes wonder, quite ignorantly, if the intuitive immediate perception of an idea, or beauty, or what will you, in some way passes on into ESP — type awareness.

Perhaps it's like dreams when we wake up and try to remember them and translate them into sequential terms. I'm thinking of those curious dreams which seem to be built up round the single incidents which wake you up.

Yet there's a lot of evidence which indicates that dreaming takes a long time. Perhaps there are both kinds.

One never actually dreams verbally does one? One hasn't an explicit account when one's dreaming; it's only afterwards when one recollects it. It's like going for a country walk — one doesn't think about it in terms of language; it's only afterwards when you describe it. I should have thought that most psychic experiences are taking place at the tacit, non-verbal level.

Absolutely; that's why one feels so foolish when trying to describe them. When one says "I said", one doesn't really mean "I said".

Do you find there are two types of dream? The type which is like looking through a newspaper, or going for a rather dull country walk; and the type which I can only describe as *real*, which *means* something, where one's getting a message, or rather becoming aware of something. I had one the other night which has been nagging at me. I wonder if anyone else has had one like it. I was going up a staircase with a white cord up the middle, and the other side of it, going up the staircase with me, was a figure in white. I looked at it and it looked at me; and we *really* knew each other. And I suddenly realised that I had never really known anything or anybody in my whole life. Not *really known*. It was the most extraordinarily blissful experience. Now I realise that there is such a thing as *really* knowing another person and being known by them — one gets an amazing sense of light, clean light.

Did it, the dream, take further the kind of rapport you spoke of in connection with your husband or was it of a different order altogether?

I haven't really worked that one out. Because although there was a very deep link between my husband and myself I didn't really know him at all, and he didn't know me. I don't know how many people do know other people. I suppose you might say that my husband and I knew little bits of each other. But this was a total knowing; it was almost like *not* seeing through the glass darkly. It may have been nothing, just a dream, but the idea that it meant something is still nagging at me.

Was this something like when you took mescalin?

I don't think so. I took mescalin as a job, to give Dr. Smythies information of the kind of experience my kind of person had under the drug. So I felt I had to go on and on however scared I was and however overwhelming it seemed. I got far enough "in" — that is the only word I can use — to feel that I was in contact with aspects of the universe — focuses of consciousness — I don't know what words to use — so that it wasn't a matter of *my* knowing *them*. One was entirely swamped by their transcendency. But one thing about the mescalin business might interest you. Under the drug, and also on another occasion as the effect of natural beauty, I got taken right *out of myself.* And in each case, I was not allowed to continue looking "up" at the transcendent — what shall I call them — entities? (Yet they were all-pervasive). Well, in each case they switched me round to face away from them, so that I could look "out" at the universe with a minute fraction of their eyes. It was astounding to look "out" with a compassion and understanding utterly beyond one's own capacity. One can't hold the attitude, of course. But one can faintly, *very* faintly, remember it, or rather an echo of it. I often wonder whether religious people ought not to pray, "Let us see with a fraction of your eyes, O Lord."

Did you feel in these moments when you were drawn out of yourself by natural beauty that you were seeing more truly than at other times?

Yes.

I'm wondering what use can be made of such experience.

I don't know — it is vivifying to feel you are part of the rest of life. There is a sense of unity; there's not that separation of everyday life. And you're invigorated.

In the dream, was it a feeling of transcendence?

No, it was a feeling of completion. A feeling of relief as though you had always been dressed in thick heavy dark clothes and you had suddenly taken them all off in the sunshine. And companionship, total companionship.

And have you felt in these moments of transcendence that there is a kind of progression in them? Do you learn a little bit more each time from them?

No, because the few I've had have been so out of my class that I couldn't pretend to say that one taught me more than another. It might be that I was a little more open on one occasion, but the difference would be in me.

Do you meet people who are frightened of their own ESP gifts?

Yes, and people are also frightened of what seems to be the presence of the departed. Then there is the problem of people who believe that mediums can communicate with the discarnate. They seem to me to be very liable to mistake what I suspect is, sometimes at least, a medium's own image-making, for reality. Everything he or she says they take as coming from the discarnate. I am not, of course, in a position to say none of it does, but very often there are obvious alternative sources: their own imagination, something they have read or heard in the past and consciously forgotten, telepathy from living people, including the expectations of their sitters. I think it may mislead people not to allow for any alternatives to discarnate communication.

Do you think it is in the same class as explanations of why people brought up in different religious traditions seem to be limited in their imagery?

Yes, but only to some extent as I suspect that most of us, if not all, are confined to the imagery which is familiar to us. And different images may stand for the same quality. For instance, the Virgin Mary, Kwan Yin and the benign aspect of Kali could all stand for love and compassion. But that is not quite what worries me about mediumship. I will give you an example. After the war I wondered what had happened to a German friend of mine, of a famous family. I feared he would have been killed by the Nazis or the Russians and I thought it would be interesting to go to a medium about him *before* trying to find out. She got his Christian name, reminded me of many happy things he had done in America with my family and said he had been killed in horrible circumstances of which he did not want to be reminded — just as I feared. The sitting was very convincing. Afterwards I tried to get news of him by ordinary means, and finally the Swiss Foreign Office traced him to Lichtenstein. He wrote to me that he was living in two rooms and had never been so happy. So the medium had got my fears, not the facts.

Do you think there is any convincing evidence of survival?

I absolutely do not know. My reasoning side finds it exceedingly difficult to envisage, but rather less so than hitherto, as nowadays so many impossibilities are turning out to be facts! But I have another side which appears, on occasion, to be contacted by my departed friends, usually when they want help given to people they loved on earth. I do not see them. Or one could say I do not make an image of them. But I feel keenly aware of their invisible but vigorous living presences. I have solved this dilemma for myself but by leaving my analytical side to doubt as much as it likes. But my intuitive, experiencing side I allow to welcome them as if they were themselves. I would rather be a fool than a knave who cuts my friends.

5

Peter Baelz

As a theologian, how do you see the relation between religious experience and theology?

I take theology in a rather narrow sense, as an interpretation of experience arising out of a specific tradition. For the theologian it's the structuring of experience that is of more importance than the experience itself. I'm not sure how far, if you start from experience, you can find categories for interpreting it which arise necessarily out of the experience itself. Much of what people talk about as religious experience, it seems to me, *can* be interpreted in a whole variety of different structural forms, either personal or impersonal.

How do you distinguish between the structure *of experience and its* content*? There seems to me to be a very intimate relationship.*

I'm not sure that one can get at the content, or speak of the content, without some structural presuppositions.

Such as?

Well, for example, when we are speaking of the content of our sense experience, whether one speaks in terms of objects, or sense data, and so on, it seems to me that the kind of structure you are using will dictate, or at least relate to, what appears actually to exist; can we get back, as it were, to the basic bricks of experience, and then see what kind of interpretation we put on them? I wonder whether this is possible; whether the very basic bricks are not in some sense determined by the kind of structure you bring to them.

Or the language which you use.

Yes, the structure is implicit in the language.

Still, unless we taken an entirely idealist view we do admit that there is an external world to be perceived.

Oh yes. Obviously the external world *is* something outside ourselves. But when we speak of experiencing "things", what counts as a "thing"? I'm not sure that a thing is not just something that can be used by us for our own purposes. There's a certain coherence about a "thing". But what are things actually made up of? I can't get to the "given" apart from some structuring. I don't want to be a 100% idealist but I'd question whether there's anything that's *purely* given.

Still, the given element is there, however hard it may be to speak of it with any precision.

Oh yes. But can you pinpoint it? Can you disentangle it? I'm not sure that you can; and this is what I want to ask, whether the process of disentangling as we call it doesn't involve some structural, conceptual apparatus.

One of the reasons why I find the study of people's reminiscences of their early childhood so interesting is that here apparently one comes across accounts of experience that were intensely vivid and meaningful, which yet occurred at an age before anything like indoctrination or cultural influence can set in. There are people who go back to the age of 2 or even earlier, and who recall moments of intense awareness, described with great conviction, of something which they knew then with absolute certainty, rather as Wordsworth did. Can one not say that these experiences are authentically, truthfully recorded? One is back at some kind of experience which is, I won't say pure content and no structure, but one in which there is a very high degree of content and a very low degree of structure. How can one assess these? Some of them are extraordinarily vivid.

But when people tell of these experiences, are they not structuring? Isn't the very telling already a structuring?

Of course they use adult language. At the age of two they could not have used the language which they do now, and they're quite well aware of that. But it appears that they had these experiences before they had any such mastery of language.

Would this kind of experience be a kind of feeling-experience: of exaltation, joy, peace?

All these terms are used. But some of them say that what they experienced was not merely a feeling but an understanding, *a sense of the intense* meaningfulness *of the world. Of course all these accounts are very vulnerable to criticism; for who is to say how authentic they are? But after reading quite a number of them the sheer accumulation becomes very convincing.*

In what sense would there be an understanding? In what sense would such experience be meaningful? Is it because it carries with it a kind of glory, which ordinary experience hasn't got, and casts light on the ordinary?

There's a very strong unitive element in them. Everything seems to be comprehended all at once. It's not the comprehension of the discursive reasoning, in which this is related to that, and so gradually an understanding is reached. Suddenly everything appears totally intelligible, totally meaningful as a whole. And sometimes of course adults describe the same sort of thing; it's not confined to the years of childhood.

I have heard from adults, from people, for example, who have undergone a bereavement of someone close to them, that they have had the feeling that "everything's all right"; that is the sort of expression. This is not a discursive understanding. It's not even I feel an "intelligibility", but rather a sense of deep assurance which embraces the disharmonies.

An assurance, yes, and often also a sense of unity, an awareness of a whole which in itself is totally comprehensible, perfectly open to the understanding.

If one asks what they have understood, what kind of answer would come? Is it that they feel they no longer want to ask questions? Or that they no longer feel anxieties? There is a kind of practical understanding, I suppose, in which questions simply drop away; one no longer feels disposed to ask questions. In that sense I can understand how an interpretation is a unification. I wouldn't want to deny the validity of this kind of experience or to question what the "cash content" of the experience is. But again I think it could be interpreted in various structures both naturalistic and theistic, or even atheistic. This is what I mean when I say that, granted these experiences are valid, I'm not sure how necessarily they lead to any kind of structure.

I'm not quite sure what you're meaning by "leading to a structure" here.

The question is, what is it they actually reveal? What do they give us understanding of?

The experiences I am interested in, and we have many good examples that illustrate it, are where people feel themselves in touch with something beyond themselves, some transcendental element whether they call it God or not, so that their whole lives are altered. The experience is such that they receive support and strength to do things they would not otherwise be capable of. They pray for an answer to their aspirations rather than their ambitions, and find it works; they are enabled to do what previously they could not. I think this kind of experience is very important. There are various names given to this power in different primitive religions: among the Polynesians it is "mana", among the North American Indians it is "wakum", and so on. Man seems to be able to be in touch with something that appears to be beyond the self. Psychologists may well say that it is an "overbelief" when people claim that it is in fact something beyond; what I am interested in is the power that such experience gives, in enabling man to do things he could not do otherwise. I think this has been tremendously important in the evolution of man. It has survival value. There is something very significant here that is at the back of all religion. It may be no more than the Jungian shared unconscious; I don't know. All I know is, from my own experience, that it does work. It's a very real power.

Couldn't it be said that these "structures" of yours are merely cultural fashions or habits of thought, and what these experiences really have in common, is not structure but content or effect?

Yes; I'm interested in this "empowering" effect. If one looks at just a human level one can sense how one can get empowered by being with a particular person. Now whether we say that the experiences are just the same, or whether the empowering by a particular person develops by a relationship between persons I'm not sure. The question really is whether these structures are just cultural ones or whether the structuring does lead to a different development of the experience, or leads it to be developed in a different direction. And if the experience arises from contact with a person rather than some natural scene or object, will the form of its development be altered? I don't want to deny that there is this very basic content of something other than ourselves empowering us; but I wonder whether the effect on ourselves, and the life which we develop in respond to this power, may be different according to the way we understand this power; just as for example the kind of life I live in relation to another person may be different from the kind of life I live in relation to an object of nature which I do not interpret in personal categories. If you interpret this power in personal terms, as purposive or caring, the kind of life you develop in relation to it may be — I'm not saying that it is — subtly different from what it would be if you interpreted it simply in impersonal language.

For myself, I think one must approach it in a personal way, for psychological reasons. I think it's bound up with the child-parent relationship, but to my mind that doesn't make it any less valid. But one may know it is not an actual person, but still feel that it corresponds to a person.

I think the question is how much emphasis do you put on this "corresponds to" a person. Even if we let go of the idea of the old gentleman in the sky, if we think of a person as being the centre of purposive activity, do we see this power as such a centre?

I'm not sure about the "purposive activity", but I am sure about the sense of response, as if it were a person responding, as if one were making contact with a person. I look upon religion as one of the most important things in biology that we haven't yet understood. Love has been developed in two main ways in the animal kingdom: in the bringing of the sexes together, which is an important mechanism in physical evolution, bringing about the shuffling of the genes, the DNA and so on. Then in the higher animals, the birds and mammals, you've got a love-relationship between parent and child which is not a sexual one. And when man first discovered a language in which to express his feelings of there being something beyond the self, it isn't surprising that it became personified by analogy with the child-parent relationship. It was felt to be something that could only be approached in some such personal way. The love-relationship is the only thing that matters really in the whole organic world.

I am very much in sympathy with what you say about these relationships in the organic world, and their biological survival value. And if we find this personal relatedness at the peak which evolution so far has reached, and if we want to go on to extend this personal relating even to this power beyond, whatever it may be, so that it would be an "as if" relationship, "as if" personal, I don't see why one shouldn't take the next step and say that this power *is* personal.

Yes I would take that step. But one needn't necessarily speak of some huge anthropomorphic object beyond ourselves.

I don't know what one would mean by "a huge anthropomorphic object beyond ourselves". I see this power as a centre of activity, a power — and I speak theologically now — which is creative, and lures into response all the independent sub-activities in the world; and I would say that the growth or response of love is to a centre of activity which is God. Whether this is an anthropomorphic concept I don't know.

I'd agree with you there; but it's talk about man being made in the image of God that worries me.

But why? Aren't you actually saying that man is in the image of God in one sense, if you say that the only possible relationship to this power is an "as if personal" one? I feel you want to have your cake, by putting in the "personal", and then withdraw it by putting the "as if" in.

Well, no, not really.

Well I know, but I'm only putting this as bluntly as I can to draw you out. If I thought I was having an "as if personal" relationship with you, and that the only way to understand you was to treat you *as if* you were a person, I'm not sure in what way that would differ from my saying that you *are* a person. Only if I suddenly discovered that you were a carefully contrived automaton which had, as it were, been fashioned by this group to deceive me — then I would say I had been hoodwinked all along.

I think it's this word "image" that gets in the way. Thought-patterns and feelings are more important. If you say that God is in the image of the soul of man I'd cheer and say, yes, I'm with you.

I think the step I'm taking is this: in the order of knowing I'd quite happily say God is made in the image of man: that in our getting to know and trying to understand and grasp what transcends us, we find the "as if personal" category works, because there's a real life that develops if we use this kind of approach; so we say therefore that God is made in the image of man. But I'd want to take a further step, and say that, in our knowing, we are responding to what in the order of being is prior to us and as it were luring our response from us, evoking it, and therefore He is the ultimate reality in the order of being, and we are being brought through the evolutionary process, through all the seeking to what we can't yet reach, towards our personal response to Him. We are being conformed as it were to God.

Would you say that the God of Australopithecus was the same as the God of Homo sapiens? Did the image change?

Well I don't know anthropologically; images have been changing and developing throughout history through different religions. There are different images of God to-day. The Muslim God for example is a God of sheer power demanding obedience (this may be a slight distortion as there are different strands in Islam); whereas as I understand it the Christian God is power interpreted in terms of caring and love; He is not the potentate, and therefore He lets me be, He lets me respond to Him, He lets me make my mistakes, He lets me search Him out; He is there inviting me.

You're not saying that the Christian God is different from the Muslim God, are you?

I'm saying that the Christian understanding is different. If there's God, there's only one God, and He's God whatever we think of Him. He is what He is, and we can't make Him any different.

Yes, I agree; and I think the understanding of Australopithecus was very different from ours. But it's the same God that's there. But it may be that God is evolving with the process of our understanding.

The *image* has been evolving; God himself may be; I am inclined to think he may be enriched by the world. If he creates the world and cares for it, then in some sense the content of his joy must be enlarged when things improve. Whatever the changelessness of God may be, there must certainly be that entering into the life of the world; he can't be purely impassible. Theologically speaking, I would say he is impassible in the sense that he is not taken by surprise. Because He is related to everything that happens, His power, His force, His presence, His guidance, His law, whatever you like to say, is in and behind the whole of the evolutionary process.

It always worries me slightly when we think of those two or two and a half thousand million years before anything like man appeared; what was God doing all that time? What are your thoughts about that? It wouldn't surprise me if there was a God of starlings, of thrushes, of blackbirds, in a sense of a shared subconscious behaviour pattern, corresponding in some way to Bergson's "élan vital".

I would have thought from the point of view of Christian theology one would have to say something like this: that He rejoices in the brute creation, that he is luring the brute creation into something more akin to his knowing, caring love.

But over so many million years.

Oddly enough this doesn't worry me.

But when you think of all the wastage and cruelty — "Nature red in tooth and claw" — of how few survive the mutual destruction of so many preying on each other.

Well yes, this is worrying; but when one comes to man, it seems that man ought to take the responsibility. I can see that in some sense this is my fault, it is due to *my* failure. One cannot say that the lower animals ought to have acted more responsibly. But I wonder whether the "red in tooth and claw" aspect of nature isn't sometimes overdone. In a sense this is built into the natural world, in which you've got systems of activity coming all the time into interaction, and in the interaction they either amalgamate or take over and become more and more complex in that way. And so as life develops you've got a similar kind of competitiveness. Perhaps naively, as a theologian I would say this is the kind of cost involved in making the kind of human beings we are.

We couldn't have appeared unless all this had gone before.

Well yes; but whether it's worth it is the question. You couldn't have had this kind of embodied feeling, conscious, knowing, caring, willing, aspiring being without all this coming before. The question to my mind would be, had I been God, would it have been worth the cost? And — this sounds terribly pietistic I'm afraid — but the way I try and think about this, the way that alleviates it a bit, is partly that I don't think God is so much at a distance, having set the whole thing going, and sitting back and watching all the time, but that He Himself is somehow involved in it all.

I think he is a striving God, working through evolution.

Peter Baelz

Yes I would agree with you; though I wouldn't want to make Him striving in the sense that He Himself is not sure where He wants to go, what He's about.

One might even speak of almost an unconscious God; is the whole business of evolution the result *of His creative work, or is it something in which He Himself is evolving too? Can one speak as Alexander did, as though God was always the next stage, in some sense, as though God were being made Himself as a part of the evolutionary process?*

No, I would want to say that God is also the already existing end of the evolutionary process; that he is calling into being through this vast expanse of time beings who can respond to Him, and can recognize Him.

If one person has experience of one kind of God, and another of a quite different kind, where is all your theology?

Well the theology is the wrestling with the question what kind of God makes most sense of the evolutionary process of nature, of the coming into being of man and of his struggle and aspiring after goodness — what kind of God makes most sense of this? I think the argument, if there *is* an argument for theism, is one that you can't easily pin down. It is ultimately the affirmation that this kind of belief makes most sense of the totality of our experience. One can give *kinds* of reasons, *kinds* of arguments for this; but in the end it's a matter of a hunch, of faith, as to where the whole thing's going to end up. I would say that in the end the outcome of this whole evolutionary process will show what it's been about.

If we try to envisage what it might be, we're only perhaps half way through the evolutionary process. Some people say it was two or three thousand million years to those first organic structures we should call life. Well before the earth cools or gets burnt up, whichever it is, we have got an almost equal stretch, unless we destroy ourselves. Can you envisage, at the rate at which we're developing, with this immense acceleration of technology, where we're going to go? We have just reached the moon. In a thousand, in ten thousand years, we shall be able to go to any of the planets. We shall also probably be able to suspend life, either by freezing or drying. And then computers will be able to answer any possible question that we can ever imagine. When you have reached that stage, you will then know how to start life again.

We are the children of God; we are becoming like God, and we may be able to create a new universe somethere out in the galaxy; and the whole object of the thing is what? — to give love and joy.

I am so unimaginative that I find it hard to stretch my imagination to envisage it all. In one sense the computers may give us the answers. But they can't be creative, and they can't tell us what we should use our knowledge for. I find it difficult to believe that we shall have changed so much that we shall no longer experience things like joy and pain.

No, I think these things are common to all animate matter; I think Joy and beauty go right through the universe. We are becoming more and more explicit, and able to express and discuss our tacit feelings of joy, beauty and love. Language and science enable us to do this; they have built up knowledge that will enable us to tell how life first began.

I wonder a bit about language being only the explicit articulation of the tacit. I wonder whether language, at least poetic language or musical language, the symbolization of our feeling, doesn't even enhance our deeper feelings. I do agree that language from time to time fails, and that silence, non-linguistic appreciation, can rise higher; but I wonder whether it would take us higher unless we also had the language in which we try to give expression to, and so come to know, the significance and meaning of so many things. I think for example that a good poem can enhance our joy and feeling of significance; and *only* those words put in that way by the poet can do that job. I have a very high regard for language, though there are times when it can be abysmally abused and we want the language just to drop away. To my mind the tacit and the explicit are subtly interwoven. The rational and the symbolic, too, the ordinary and the extraordinary are closely woven together. If I could understand more of what you scientists do, I feel my appreciation of the world around me would be greater. Language has these two functions, to enable us both to understand and to appreciate. Love and wisdom, love and truth — I want to find them together.

I'm afraid I have a very prosaic mind, and all these speculations about the nature of God and the possibility of our understanding Him — to me this is the kind of thing that brings theology into bad repute. But if all our understanding of God and all our theorizing about Him originally comes from our own experience, surely it is here that we must start. I find all these speculations leave me cold. As has already been asked, if one person has an experience of God in one form, and another an experience in another form, who is to decide between them? The philosopher may say that we must decide which of these experiences makes better sense of the whole world; but for the particular person at the particular moment his experience is *revelatory; it* does *make sense.*

There is a continuing shaping of the world, and a continuing shaping of human nature in reaction to the world; and one tries to interpret and set side by side this experience and that one. The desire to understand, to see life whole, to see the unity, is something very deep in man. And therefore as he continues, and as new experiences come upon him, his previous understanding and interpretation is going to be modified. Therefore there will grow up a tradition, I would want to argue, religious traditions, Christian, Buddhist, Islamic and so on, which have a reasonableness, in the sense that they attempt to present a coherent view of the world, but which also can and will illuminate the individual's experience. I have no desire to hand over to you a packet of theology; it won't do you any good. But it might possibly be the truth that in this packet there is an understanding of the world that is the result of numerous people's experience and reflection, criticized, changed, modified, built up over the years. So, while some individuals may still want to start from scratch, and very rightly, because everyone has to start with his own experience, yet the tradition, *if* it is a living tradition and that's a very big if, will perhaps enable him to say, "Yes, I can see my experience in these terms; so I can expect this, and look for that". He finds a ground. The trouble is when a tradition becomes purely dead and formal and speculative. In a sense all theology is speculative, in that it tries to think things together; but it shouldn't be speculative in the sense of having nothing to do with people's experience.

One does get the impression that what a lot of theologians are really writing about is just theology. In fact a certain professor of theology in this University is on record only last year as defining theology as "what theologians do when they are doing theology".

Yes, and G. E. Moore was once asked what philosophy was, and he scratched his head and pointed round to all the books on his shelves, and said, "That's philosophy". This is a sort of professional answer. In the long run it won't do. I think in fact there are theologians who are worried about the status of theology. Quite obviously it is problematic in a way in which science is not problematic; so they look at themselves and at what they are doing, and try to say what theology is. I would want to say, in the larger sense, that it is interpretation of experience; and that there are various modes and levels of interpretation of experience. Of these science is one, and art is another and theology is yet another — and one which hopes to be the most inclusive. But if it doesn't make sense of people's experience I think this is a prima facie objection to it.

It does at times seem that theologians are a little patronizing. They are in the habit of saying to people who describe their experiences in their own terms, "Ah yes, what you are really saying is this"*; and then they will offer a theological interpretation.*

For example, a person writes in to us saying they have experienced a sense of a very comforting presence. What need is there for a further interpretational structure?

Well even that phrase — experiencing a sense of presence — is in a way interpretative. If you feel somebody is there, you have already got the notion of somebody; you are already applying the category of a human being which you have got from ordinary experience to interpret this feeling of presence. Supposing I hadn't been in contact with any human being, I couldn't have said, "I feel someone is there". It's not a conscious interpretation.

But to have had previous experience of the presence of human beings doesn't provide one with a structure of interpretation for what is really quite a different experience.

Yes, but as soon as you put it into language, and you try and identify the experience for yourself, the interpretative process beings. All languages are social constructs; there may not be any deliberate act of interpretation involved, but it does seem that when we use a language, we are making use of a way we have learnt to speak of or single out this or that particular kind of experience, to identify it.

Well even if there is an element of interpretation in all our description of experience, this doesn't always justify the very complicated and sophisticated interpretative structure that theologians offer us to describe our experience. There is a revolt, isn't there, against what I would call the patronage of theology. When the theologian says, in effect, "what you're really talking about is this", *a chap may say, "well, I don't see that it is at all; all I experienced was* this". *Some theologians even seem to imply that we don't need experience, when we ought to know that the truth is thus and thus.*

Well I've never come across theologians who really said that, because even revelation depends upon experience. When you listen to someone declaring something to be true, it involves the experience of deciding whether he is trustworthy or not.

Still, one does sometimes feel that theologians are living in a world of their own, a kind of Platonic world of eternal certainties, while down here we are working with people who have no contact with this world of theology, but nevertheless have these experiences for which they have no language at all. They are groping around in the darkness, and often succeeding, very vividly, in describing these experiences in totally untheological language. There is a great rift here. Six hundred years ago the Church provided language that they felt acceptable. Now this is no longer generally so.

It saddens me to think that theologians simply feel you are wasting your time. It's stupid of theologians if they believe that these experiences are of no importance or significance. If there is a real experience, one that changes a person's life for the better, I was going to say thank God — or thank Nature — for it! This kind of experience has obviously played a large part in the development of a religious life — a life of which theology attempts to give as consistent and coherent an interpretation as it possibly can. This may be just my own horrid intellectualism, because I do lack experience of this kind of thing; how does it relate to other kinds of experience, ordinary, humdrum ones or tragic ones? Do they fit together at all? One may say, "No; life is just a succession of different kinds of experience. Some people may have had these saving or releasing experiences, and had their lives changed, but that is all there is to be said about it." I think where the theologian comes in — as does the old-fashioned kind of metaphysician — is to ask: "Does this kind of experience, along with our ordinary or tragic or other kinds of experience, help us to some insight or understanding of what the ultimate, one hopes perhaps the unifying, meaning of life is? Of what Reality is?"

Maslow has a nice phrase: he talks about "helium-filled words" — words which rise gently above the earth, and continue to float away, beyond all contact with this world as we know it.

Could you give us an example?

You've been listening to examples all this evening!

You see we get some people who write in, I am sure in total sincerity, describing perfectly genuine experiences, and they go on about sin, salvation, redemption and so on, using all the old theological clichés, and these, to many people, are totally "helium-filled".

Well all words are "helium-filled", and this goes for all your scientific language as well, unless they relate to something that you've experienced or understood. I agree with you that all these terms can take on a life of their own; theology does sometimes seem to me to be no more than a theological word-game. You make one move, and you know what the next one will be. But I believe that these words like sin and forgiveness do have an experiential basis or relevance. And I hope that when I use the words — well I try to keep them earthed. I think they can be earthed; some people do feel they know what sin and forgiveness mean. Whether they are right or not is another matter. But I only have to look across the road to St. Aldate's: they would tell me there.

How do you look forward to the future of natural theology?

What exactly does one mean by "natural theology"? That out of one's own experience of nature there arises a theology? Or does one mean a theology of nature? In this there would be a continuing interplay between our experiences of nature and evolution and so on, a reaching out towards something that is new, the idea of the personal perhaps, which then reflects upon and integrates what we have already learnt. I find this distinction between "natural" and "revealed" rather artificial.

I see natural theology as a study of this transcendental type of experience as recorded by so many people; it's a study of this, linked with anthropology, psychology and biology. I think natural theology has a long way to go before it becomes a science; it's got to go through a period of "natural history" for a long time. (For one thing we've got to get a good deal further in the field of certain aspects of parapsychology.) Then it may be as respectable as any other branch of science. That would be the only respectable kind of theology, if I may say so: a science of God, based on human experience.

Peter Baelz

Yes, this sounds to me entirely proper and right. How exactly it is going to work out I'm not sure. In one sense the experience of God, as it develops, may involve certain attitudes or beliefs about God, just as our experiencing of other people involves our gaining certain beliefs about them as we develop an understanding of them.

Yes, but one must always be ready to discard them. The history of science has been full of beliefs which have been discarded. I'd like to see a progressive natural theology that would not be worried about throwing over dogmas in favour of new ones suggested by psychology, sociology, anthropology and so on. One should not want a theology based on any dogmatic system.

Yes, I would have said that if there are good reasons for overthrowing certain dogmatic beliefs they ought to be overthrown. In that sense I'm a natural theologian. But what is to count as a good reason? What counts as a good reason for overthrowing the basic presuppositions of science? This is what puzzles me about certain parapsychological phenomena. It's not that, in a sense, they are not real. But how can the whole structure of science, which has been so fruitfully built up, integrate them?

Well, clearly there are a great many well-established phenomena that cannot be integrated into any materialistic scientific structure: the phenomena of hypnosis and suggestion, for example, which raise the whole question of the mind-body relationship. A great deal of currently held scientific theory will have to be modified if we are to come to terms with things like these.

Haven't we totally left out of our discussion so far the history of religious experience? Surely it is not only present-day beliefs and feelings that can be regarded as valuable. The whole legacy of the past is, at least potentially, part of our present experience. History seems to me to be unlike science in this respect; there is no progressive building up of a body of agreed knowledge, by a process in which false or the inadequate ideas are gradually replaced by the true or more satisfactory.

I have always assumed that our historical experience is as much part of our experience as our immediate experience. I mean the traditions into which we have entered, the insights of other people we have trusted and on the basis of which we have advanced, even if there comes a time when we have to question them. Man's growing into a person depends upon this historical movement, not only of the individual from birth to death but of the individual in relation to the insights and tradition and values which he has received and into which he enters from past history. In that sense the Christian tradition is heavily dependent — let's put it in these terms, though they're terribly heretical — on the experience of God given to Jesus: that something here hit him and hit those who were his disciples that seemed to them of tremendous significance for interpreting man's response to the transcendent; and that in history therefore we have these moments in which exceptional things happened. Because of what they have contributed, we do see further, see deeper.

I certainly would not want to discard all that the past has to offer and in particular the whole Christian tradition. But it must be subject to continual reinterpretation. Take the case of the appearances of the resurrected Christ. We have so many very similar cases where people known to be dead have appeared in a totally convincing form to those who knew them when alive. There are obvious analogies here. And anyway, as biologist I cannot accept the idea of a physical resurrection of a material body.

Well the Gospel writers did insist that what was seen of Jesus was not a ghost. But I wouldn't particularly want to argue against your point of view on apparitions.

Perhaps one could here make the point that nothing in history has yet finally happened. There is no single event in the past whose influence we can say is now exhausted. There is nothing in history that is not always open to reinterpretation; it is not crystallized. Perhaps the same should be said of theological beliefs.

I think this is true in two senses. There is an eschatological element in all Christian doctrine; it looks to an end, a completion. It's *that* that will show what all nature, all history have been about. The Christian view is that in Jesus we have some anticipation of what its all going to be shown to have been about. The other thing is that we just don't know what we are going to become; but from a Christian point of view there is an assurance that whatever we shall become we shall be like Him, in the sense that here is the pattern, the goal to which the whole of creation is being called. So Christian theology at its best has an openness to the future, but an openness that is not without some sense of anticipated direction.

Some of us who are faced with the problems of putting over these ideas, this tradition, to those to whom it is entirely unfamiliar, in the educational context for example, do feel at times a certain despair when they contemplate the problems of communication that arise. One sometimes feels the need to lower one's sights pretty drastically.

I may sometimes feel despair about the difficulty of the job, but I don't despair of its appropriateness. Theology is the attempt to think about and see together, to get an overall understanding if you like; it seeks to relate whole masses of experience, religious experience, historical experience and so on. The Christian faith dares to say that it has some grasp, it has been given some understanding, of the coherence, the cohesion of it all. The theologian has to ask, does my theology make these experiences — taken as real — does it relate them intelligibly to this, that and the other? And the other question is, do these experiences, taken at their phenomenological level, raise any questions about my theological interpretations? I feel the danger is that the two bits have come apart.

When you talk of theology relating whole masses of experience, religious, historical and so-on, it reminds me of its old claim to be "Queen of the Sciences". Do you still see it as something like that?

I wouldn't say it was a science in the way we use that word now. But a queen, possibly, yes, in the constitutional sense, in that it doesn't (or shouldn't) dictate to experience to tell it what it's all about, but says rather, "Look, in the constitution here's how we fit together". Not an authoritarian queen. Or do you still feel there's a great divide?

I just have a great sympathy for all these people who have had intensely vivid and meaningful experience, perhaps over a whole lifetime, for the interpretation of which they find no help in any theology. There is a complete break in the tradition. There's a similar break in the tradition of Christian art. Most modern Church art is either drearily derivative or it's kitsch. This means that people to whom it comes most naturally to express their religious ideas in some visual or tangible form have no contemporary language, and without it they are lost. The same may well be true for some people who search for verbal ways of expressing their feelings. All they are offered are these words that float up into the clouds.

Peter Baelz

Well half of me, perhaps 51% of me, or 49% on Tuesdays, Thursdays and Saturdays, is in exactly that position. But there's another half of me that still finds meaning and practical significance bearing upon life in the tradition. I live with one foot in both these worlds. Sometimes I swing over on one side, sometimes I swing back onto the other. (What day of the week is it today?) If we feel able to sympathize and identify with both, it's worth trying to see whether the two do come together at all, or what it is that won't let you let either go. I know many of my colleagues both in and outside the Church live in the same position. Even if I don't like it I can't pretend it isn't true. But I'm not prepared at the moment to drop the old tradition, because I have a hunch that there's a great amount of truth in it.

6

Monica Furlong

There seem to be some people to whom religious experience comes in a series of flashes or individual moments of insight; whereas others record nothing of this kind at all, but seem to be aware throughout their lives of a kind of pull, a steady influence which they feel to be religious or transcendental, without ever having any such moments of ecstasy or special insight. But I suspect that this is really a quite artificial division.

It may be that those who have had these particular ecstatic or extraordinary experiences are those who have a resistance to having such experience all the time. Perhaps they store up experience until it explodes in some way that is so obvious that they can't act as if it hadn't happened. I am myself the sort of person who has had this sudden, explosive kind of experience; but also I think I'm someone who finds it hard to experience; I can only experience something that happens in such an extreme form that I'm then quite sure it's happening. I've experimented a certain amount with hash, and I find it hard to be absolutely sure that something unusual is happening; whereas others who are having the same kind of hash at the same time are able to have experiences, and to be unafraid or unashamed of having them.

You mean the pressure builds up?

Yes. I think so.

Why should some people deny having had such experiences?

I think it's to do with being afraid of letting go, or wanting to be in control of the situation; so you don't want any outside experience to come in and take away your control.

Do you think this is due to some kind of cultural disapproval?

Yes, I should think so. It's all to do with the growing process, and in this one learns to know where one can feel safe, and this lies in doing what society expects of you. This makes it very difficult to have these other kinds of experiences which you haven't been trained to handle.

I was thinking of those kinds of societies in which these "explosive" experiences seem to be relegated to a special sort of person, like the Shamans. With us I suspect there's a general tendency to suppress such feelings as these.

I can't say it's something I've given a great deal of thought to. If one is going to have experiences of this extraordinary kind I suppose they do set up a certain anxiety.

If we do come to terms with such experiences, or are courageous in facing up to them, does this mean that we shall then be more open to all sorts of other things that at present we are not aware of?

I think what is hard, at least in our sort of society, is on the one hand to be open to all kinds of strange experiences, and on the other to be able to cope with ordinary everyday life. We seem to be split up into those who can cope with the everyday and those who can explore by means of these unusual experiences.

In many societies there is, or was, a conscious polarization here: in African village societies certain people were regarded as separate, or different, they were the kind of people for whom it was normal to have contact with the unseen world, leaving the rest of us to get on with our ordinary daily life. They were rather like lightning conductors. There was a kind of division of labour. This is surely a feature not just of primitive societies, but of our contemporary western culture too?

Yes.

Looking at it from a psychological point of view we might perhaps say that everybody has something of these feelings but they prefer to project them on to somebody else because they can't cope with them. So society has actually set up people whom we can project these feelings onto and then pretend they (the feelings) are nothing to do with us. They become holy men. We ourselves don't want to be holy, so we have holy men on whom to project that part of us that does wish to be holy. I wonder if it follows that the person who is capable of continuous experience throughout life, as opposed to the occasional explosive experience, is someone who has achieved a mature personality; the person who can cope with such experience regularly has something that other people don't.

I don't think it works out quite like that. It seems to me that, in our society at any rate, a person is only able to have extraordinary experiences through having somehow at an earlier stage of life repressed some of the more normal experiences; while those who are able to experience ordinary human things to the full are only able to do so through repressing some of these extraordinary experiences. I don't think that either group is wholly unable to have the experiences that the other half does; it's just that somehow or at some time each has opted for one set or another. What I hope can happen in our society, and I think perhaps there are signs of it, is that each of these groups will become able to experience some of the things which hitherto they have been unable to; so that we shan't have these two extremes. I'd like the whole thing to get kind of stirred in, so that the saints become a bit closer to their fellow human beings and vice versa.

I should like to think that if we can get sufficient evidence of this feeling of being in touch with something that appears to be beyond the self, a great many people who for cultural reasons may have suppressed this feeling will acknowledge it, or at any rate give it a trial.

Yes; though actually the suppression I was thinking of is one that generally occurs at an earlier stage than that of deciding whether you are going to be able to explain what you have experienced. Even in the African societies mentioned earlier, it is as if in an early stage of people's development they have settled either for being holy and extraordinary or for just being ordinary.

This experience of being in touch with something transcendental is common to many primitive peoples. As Marrett says, it is a kind of ability to make contact with something that alters the tribal luck. This seems to be something important from a biological point of view; there's a reality here, a sort of spiritual know-how that we can make use of.

But in our relatively sophisticated society are we to go on expecting certain individuals to have certain experiences and the rest of us not to, or only to have them second-hand through them? Or are we going to expect everyone to start having them? This is to me the really interesting question.

There seems to be a suggestion here that those of us who have repressed these feelings will be as it were, tone-deaf, when it comes to extraordinary experiences; whereas those of us who, for whatever reason, have had a more liberated kind of upbringing will not suffer that kind of disability.

I don't think it is a question of having had a liberated upbringing or not. It is rather that this is an age that represses transcendence, and with some of us that repression hasn't wholly succeeded.

Perhaps, if we are to use Freudian language, we should speak of suppression as well as repression. Repression is an unconscious process; but there is a great deal of conscious suppression going on. Our whole educational system suppresses ideas which make us feel uncomfortable and rewards the kind of person who is good at controlling his environment and is quick at learning to master the techniques of material life. It does not reward the dreamer. Surely this is a quite conscious process.

Yes, very true.

And in fact this suppression is unsuccessful; it is those whose early environment is very suppressive who experience things later on; they have just had to break down in some way. It is those of us who have had a more ordinary, run-of-the-mill kind of suppressive background who are the ones who don't see.

Yes, it is the extreme suppression that becomes so utterly intolerable that something has to explode and break through.

But then when it does come out with such violence it is so easy to discuss it as pathological or abnormal.

For the observer yes; but for the person it's happening to, it may not be so easy.

But society encourages us to view it as abnormal.

Yes.

Jung's theory of psychological types may be helpful here. He would say that we have learnt to experience in certain ways through our dominant personality function, whether it is thought, feeling, intuition or sensation; whereas more experience may come through our inferior function; and if only one becomes aware of what is one's inferior side one will understand better what is coming in.

Yes, I would agree with that. But you've still got to account for these sudden explosive experiences and explain them to yourself somehow.

How would you account for the apparent fact that these experiences which we have called "explosive" are more common in childhood and adolescence than in later life? Is it perhaps that by adulthood we have developed a thicker skin, a protective carapace?

Yes. I had a kind of conversion experience in adolescence, and then as so often happens this was sort of overlaid. Then when I was 36 I took LSD, and really just the same sort of experience as I had at the time of my conversion, only in a considerably stronger form, was started off. It was really exactly the same kind of experience. I could see that I had reached the stage where, if I hadn't taken LSD, I simply shouldn't have been able to experience it, because such a lot of other things had happened and come in between me and the original experience.

Do you still regard that conversion experience of your adolescence as having been something genuine and valuable at the time, or is it something you regret?

What I do regret is that, because of other things that had happened during adolescence, I had to experience it in that sort of extreme form. If other things had happened in the way they should have done, then all the things I had through that conversion experience I should have been able to experience in ordinary ways. As it was, the pressure built up and I had to have the experience in an explosive form. But I think I had to have that experience somehow.

Do you think if you hadn't had that earlier experience the LSD experience would not have done as much for you? It was perhaps only uncovering what was in a sense already there.

It's very hard to say, because the conversion experience set off a whole lot of other experiences — all of which in some form I also experienced under LSD. One cannot say if one had not had that earlier chain of experiences whether under LSD one could have even understood what was happening to one at all.

But you did say that the later LSD experience was exactly the same as the earlier one?

Well not exactly the same in content but the same in quality. But it was a considerably stronger experience because I was older and had by then experienced all sorts of other things which also came into it.

For those of us who hadn't been through an adolescent experience of that intensity, do you suppose that LSD would have had a similar kind of effect? Would it have awakened us to something latent within ourselves?

I would think so, though I really haven't sufficient experience of what happens to people under LSD. Some people seem to be describing hideous experiences — and mine was hideous in some ways — and others describe something quite different. I suppose this is why people have such anxieties over LSD; all kinds of things can happen; there is no control.

Would you say there was an element of recognition in your LSD experience, in the sense that you felt yourself to be revisiting familiar ground?

I suppose what I was hoping when I took it (though I don't think I really understood this; it only occurred to me afterwards) was that, after some sixteen years when so much of the earlier hopefulness had died away, it might confirm some of the things that had seemed so easy to understand under the influence of conversion. So one could say that, if one takes LSD in the hope of experiencing certain things, one does in fact stand a pretty good chance of experiencing them.

Could there be any other way through to rediscovering this sort of experience? Could one through meditation arrive at the same kind of end?

Yes, I think so. I am convinced that there are all sorts of other ways.

But might it take the LSD trip to trigger off the other possibilities.

Well, it certainly did for me, but I don't think it has always to be like that. Of course one can only speak for oneself and for other people it could be very different. But I think I was awfully afraid of the sort of transcendental experiences I'd had, afraid of being eaten up by them, afraid perhaps of going into some kind of schizophrenic state. And, therefore, there was a tendency to balance the scales on the other side, to do things which offered a kind of escape from this transcendental experience. This goes back to what I was saying at the beginning, that certain people only experience these things in an explosive form because they aren't able to experience them in an ordinary form. But if all the while I had been able to accept transcendental experience instead of being afraid of it, then perhaps I should never have got to the state where I felt I had to take LSD in order to explode the whole thing, and to start something happening again. I felt I'd got stuck, and certainly LSD is a very good way of getting unstuck; but it's like castor oil or epsom salts, something you only have to resort to when other things have gone wrong.

I'm very interested in what might be called a problem of identification. I was talking to a minister some months ago and he said there was no religious experience that had any validity unless it was first-hand of God. This sounds fine; but I'm sure that there are lots of people who do, in fact, lead what they would feel to be religious lives without ever having had any such first-hand experience of God, but having had it second-hand by identifying with other people who had had it first-hand, whether by reading books or by meeting people, by being able to say, "Yes, I can see what you mean; I can see you have had this experience, and I feel that it is true though I haven't had it myself." This seems a perfectly valid form of experience, and one that helps people to make sense of the world. Would you say then that there can be valid religious experience which is second-hand?

I have always felt that there are people whose early experiences of love and family life have been generally satisfactory, and that therefore they don't have to hunt for love in these strange and extreme forms; that somehow it is inside them rather than outside them. In that case I don't think the experience actually is second hand. I feel that William James' distinction between the "once-born" and the "twice-born" is unfair to the once-born; he seems to regard them as inferior, but I don't think they are inferior. They have got something inside them that the twice-born haven't got at all.

If this is true, that those who have been unhappy have to look outside themselves to find something through which they can experience the transcendent, whereas those who have been happy find it in some inner way — what does this tell us about the nature of the transcendent, the nature of God?

I think all it means is that in the end, if you don't experience things one way you'll experience them in another; which is a hopeful thought really, because wherever you start from you won't end up by being deprived.

It would certainly be neat if one found a pattern like this: that people who had had a childhood that was unsatisfactory in some way, lacking perhaps in warm personal relationships, would experience transcendence rather in relationship to abstract things, in feelings about nature or art rather than in the sense of a personal presence or father-figure.

But if they hadn't experienced such a warm personal relationship, wouldn't that be what they would be trying to experience later on?

You mean they would experience that kind of relationship just because they wanted to?

Yes, but I wouldn't for that reason regard their experience as illusory. I feel that human relationships are a reflection of some other sort of relationship, and you can either start at the human end and experience it there, or you can start at the other end and experience it there. So the whole thing adds up to a single whole. I really can't bring myself to feel that because people have a strong wish to experience something and then experience it this therefore shows that it isn't a valid form of experience.

The wish might influence the form that an experience takes, but not its content or validity?

Yes, quite.

Do you think that, if you get to the same point through meditation as you can by LSD, people have got to be prepared for it to be a long process or discipline?

I think some people rather enjoy long-drawn-out processes of discipline and other people can't stand them. So to each according to his means.

But is it as simple as that? Just technology for one, meditation for another — isn't there something about the means that in some way influences or enhances the end?

Well, I don't have any of the anti-LSD feelings that many people have, except that I'm sure people ought to do such things under supervision just to save themselves from the more frightful kind of experiences;

because I don't really think, unless people are in a certain sort of state when they can expose themselves to these chemical experiments, that they are going to have certain kinds of experience. I think if you are sick when you take LSD you will probably have a very sick kind of experience; and if you were a saint (if such things exist — I'm very uncertain of the word "saint" these days) perhaps what you experienced would be what you always experience.

In the context of religious education, there's a great taboo on teaching children to pray; you can do that in church perhaps, but not in a state school. Do you think a case could be made for giving out hash to a small group, in a controlled way, to induce the kind of experiences to which at that age they might be sensitive, and which, classically, would have been induced by prayer?

But I don't think one ought to have hash at that age; adolescence is its own hash. One is being so exposed to all kinds of strange inner experiences in adolescence that to take drugs as well would only be to confuse and complicate things. I don't think they should be allowed drugs at that age; they should be given to you when you're about 35; that's the age when people are getting anxious for spiritual help of some kind.

I know it's commonly believed that adolescence is a time of great turmoil, which of course in many ways it is. But to judge from the people who have written to us, adolescence doesn't seem to be a time of much greater spiritual experience or insight or growth than, for example, the period between 5 and 9.

But I thought there were figures to show that conversion experiences were generally expected to happen between the ages, say, of 13 to 25.

Conversion I think involves decision, it involves the ability to think, it involves a certain power of conceptualization, doesn't it? The ability to say, "This is what I believe"?

But the fact that people at any rate used to have conversion experiences within these years suggests a certain vulnerability at this age to this kind of experience. But I wasn't thinking specifically of religious things, but to aesthetic experiences, sensitivity to poetry and music and such things.

Of course its very fashionable to decry adolescent conversion as a valuable experience. You may say people are then more "vulnerable"; you might equally well say they are more "open" at this stage. Is it right to pour scorn, as so many do, on conversion experiences in adolescence? Isn't there perhaps here something valuable?

Oh yes, I do think it's valuable. The thing that makes it harder for us to think of it in quite the same way people once did is that we now see that the guilt-feelings of adolescence, particularly sexual guilt, used to help trigger off the old-style conversion experience. Guilt-feelings got you into such a state of anxiety that something else had to happen.

I wonder whether the conversion experience as a recognizable syndrome or event occurs in societies which are basically religious? You might perhaps regard this particular experience as an inevitable product of a society, and even more of an educational system, which suppresses or, at any rate, discourages spiritual adventure, spiritual awareness, the creative imagination; so that after childhood when education really begins seriously to set in and we are encouraged to learn the kind of skills that enable us to control our environment, and when what geologists would call a "hard pan" begins to form over our intuitive and spiritual faculties — there are then some lucky people who manage to break through this crust, by means of what we see as adolescent conversion. Is this conversion in fact any more than a symptom of a rather unhealthy society, showing the need to get back to something more wholesome?

I would agree that in an ideal society people would not need conversion experiences.But this would be a society which was ideal both in its understanding of the transcendental and of people's sexual development as well. In England at any rate the times when the conversion experience had been most marked have been times when people did have tendencies to be very sexually repressed also; so that sex and religion combined to produce a very explosive force.

I wonder how far adolescent conversion experiences were characteristic of mediaeval Christendom.

Yes, it's something you hardly hear of, but in those days of course, people found it easier to have some sort of group experience, of ecstasy or excitement, which we don't find easy; perhaps we are just now beginning to be able to do it. And also at that time people didn't have such a strong sense of themselves as individuals, with their own individual difficulties and problems; they felt themselves very much more as part of a group.

In what ways do you feel that the conversion experience has anything in common with the experience of sex?

Well certainly sexual experience doesn't seem to come into the LSD experience in any way.

Timothy Leary gives very much the opposite impression.

Well there are lots of other people who have written on the subject who don't feel as he does. I think there are two ways in which sex is related to religion. One is the feeling of guilt, which certainly used to play a very big part in precipitating the conversion experience. Then there is the sense of ecstasy which people can have through sexual experience, and also through religious and group experience, as well as through taking drugs. Then the question arises, are all these forms of ecstasy really the same thing or are they all quite different kinds of experience? I feel myself that all forms of ecstasy are really aspects of the same thing. I don't think you can distinguish between some forms which you regard as acceptable and respectable and others which aren't. It is really the unification experience people hanker after.

Ecstasy can be dangerous in some forms.

It can, but it can be dangerous to be unable to experience it. If people are wholly unable to experience ecstasy then their lives become completely without interest. It is only because people hope to experience ecstasy, or have once experienced it, that their lives seem to them worth going on with. On the other hand if one's always experiencing ecstasy it becomes such a threat to one's grasp of things that one becomes hardly able to keep going at all.

And it can become addictive; one can get hooked on it. Once one has tasted this extraordinary experience one may ask, "What on earth am I doing sitting here doing 'A Levels'?"

This, of course, is the danger in taking LSD; everything ordinary and everyday just seems to become a total waste of time; it's just too much trouble to get up or keep oneself clean or anything. And this is true of all things that seem to take one up to a transcendental level; they can so easily be used as an escape from having to keep on with the everyday things. But equally, human beings seem to need them, to inspire them to keep on with the everyday. Steering a path between these two extremes is the difficult thing. And this is something that the Church has until recently seemed to do with a kind of skill, on the one hand trying to stop people having transcendental experiences, and on the other hand helping them to do so. I have a sense that it may not be able to do this any longer.

Where a church or a community through its tradition fails to be able to give any kind of guidance in this way, a tremendous weight, a tremendous strain is thrown on individuals who are left to themselves to make decisions.

Yes.

Is this perhaps why today there is this great efflorescence of cults, which seem to offer a kind of authority?

Yes, I'm sure it is.

And then our whole educational system operates purely at the level of thought. There is no attempt through education to help people manage their feelings. And I suspect it is the same in families. Families are not good at helping the growing adolescent to manage and express feeling. So what agencies are there to help people have this kind of experience?

If it is really the case that for most people today the Church and LSD are the only alternatives if they are looking for ecstasy, it is bound to be very much a minority experience. But I suspect that a form of ecstasy may be available in involvement in such things as soccer matches and other group experiences.

I'm not sure that it's really the function of the Church or the school to "set up" ecstatic experiences. But if you have ecstatic experiences what you then want is some sensible authority to come back to, so that you can say, "Look, I've had this extraordinary experience; is it OK?" Then the authority can say, "Well, you think this is extraordinary, but it isn't all that extraordinary; lots of other people have experienced it"; so that the person doesn't feel totally on his own, or on the verge of schizophrenia.

There are, of course, an increasing number of people around today, and this not only among the drug-culture, among whom these things are accepted.

Yes, they are accepted; but acceptance is not quite the same as being able to turn to someone who's a good bit further on than you are; someone who has seen all this through and come out to something on the other side.

And can put it into a wider setting, too; the trouble about the so-called "youth culture" is that they accept this kind of thing as the only *valid experience.*

Yes.

A curious kind of sentimentality persists about this among people who have gone through it. It is not felt as an ongoing, developing transforming experience, but rather as something which is looked back to with affection which from time to time may be conjured up by the playing of some old rock music or something that recreates the old atmosphere. It is something that is there for the moment; I don't see any growth, any development within the youth culture, any programme.

Yes, but this is such an early stage; you have got to hang on for another 30 or 40 years and see what these people will be like as they grow older.

The same is true perhaps of the adolescent conversion experience.

Yes; perhaps the interesting thing about conversion is what you do with it when the enthusiasm is over.

Some of our most interesting letters come from people who have had such experience when young, and felt that it was inadequate or even totally rejected it; and yet either in spite of it or through it come to some more peaceful kind of understanding. But then we don't hear from the ones who have permanently rejected it; and they may be very numerous.

Yes.

Do you think there is any social element, or consequence, of ecstasy which may make it shareable?

Certainly I would find it very difficult to translate it in any obvious or straightforward way. I don't know if you've read Saul Bellow's book *Mr. Sammler's Planet;* it's about a Polish Jew in New York. He's had all sorts of hideous experiences during the war, and one or two ecstatic ones, and has reached a stage where he can hear all the things that are happening to him, and see all the signs of pollution and violence and despair and decay, and can see on all sides people of different ages trying, in their attempts to escape from the frightful situation in which they find themselves, to find instant answers; and he just can't accept any of the instant answers, because when he compares them to the things that have happened to him they really won't stand up. And his answer, which isn't anything that I could start to imitate, is a taking of all these paradoxical things into himself without being destroyed or plunged into despair by them. If ecstasy has any value at all it must be as an assurance that on the far side of all the most frightful ups and downs one is constantly experiencing there is something else — that one can hold on to. There's something about suffering too; in one way it's just as awful as one always thinks it is, yet on a different level it isn't awful at all, so that it isn't quite what one thinks it is. And I think if we can see this then it ought to alter our view of society in some way: we would then stop squandering all our energies trying to set up a society in which we try to stop anyone suffering at any time, which we will never succeed in doing. I can't myself go to the other extreme of totalitarianism, where it's not very important if thousands of people suffer, but then I'm not sure that I'm a very political animal.

There was a sort of political ecstasy in the sort of mass demonstrations that brought Hitler to power; people can get worked up into a kind of mass hysteria of an almost ecstatic type.

Yes.

There's always the danger that unsympathetic people may regard individual ecstasy as no more than a kind of self-indulgence.

Well I suppose if it helps to keep people going and prevents them having to rely on tranquillizers or be in and out of hospital, it may be a form of self-indulgence, but it's one that fulfils a very useful function. If people find life worthwhile and satisfactory, it may stop them doing all kinds of destructive things to each other.

Would you agree that there are perhaps two things in ecstasy? One is the sudden loss of ego-boundaries, but isn't there also something coming towards you as it were from outside?

I suppose it does come from outside, but I think it comes from inside and outside at the same time; perhaps that's your "loss of ego-boundaries". There's also a sacrificial element; this is something that artists and writers feel. They experience this sort of unification and loss of self, but up to the time they reach that point there is an awful sense of having to sacrifice something in themselves. We're so stuck on the idea that ecstasy means people actually enjoying themselves and all that, that we forget that it has a sacrificial side. You do have, so to speak, to give yourself up if you want to experience ecstasy.

Hillman has something to say about this in his book Suicide and the Soul; *people who feel themselves on the verge of losing themselves in this way get tremendous suicidal tendencies.*

Yes.

But to many people who have experiences that they would call ecstatic the only really important thing is the awareness of something that is coming to them from beyond: for them ecstasy is a form of knowledge, and compared with this nothing else really matters. When you turn on a radio set you can say there is something happening inside as well as outside, but it's what is happening outside that is the important thing. And many people who have ecstatic religious experience will say that the whole cause of the thing is something well beyond themselves.

Yes; but William James also speaks of self-surrender as being an essential element.

But a surrender to something which is not of the self.

I think he thinks of it as reaching a point when you just can't any longer handle the situation; you can't keep it under control so you're open to anything that happens. I can't myself see how the giving up of control that occurs during a conversion experience relates to the kind of loss of control in the kind of political situation we were speaking of just now. There must be some overlap between the two things. One can obviously give oneself up to what is beyond one and then go on to do very evil things.

Surely there is danger in elevating this giving up of control into a virtue without any kind of discrimination.

Well actually giving up isn't as easy as all that. Perhaps people talk about it such a lot because in fact they find it quite hard to do.

This does at times bring one very much up against the problem of evil.

I suppose we're going to have to think a lot harder about the question whether evil and good are two quite separate things or whether they aren't really very closely intertwined. If you emphasize one you seem in a way to strengthen the other. Perhaps we shall have to get over our feeling that the ecstasy of the Nazi rally is quite a different thing from the ecstasy of the conversion experience; and if we don't think they are different we must see what they each have to do with the other.

One can of course get something approaching ecstasy in a great many different circumstances. I'm thinking of the scientist or the mathematician who suddenly gets a hunch; for a moment the whole thing is illumined in a remarkable way.

You mean a kind of unifying experience?

Yes; and you get something very similar in the experience of the creative artist. Also, of course, in "nature mysticism". There is the extreme kind of Wordsworthian experience in which everything merges into a single vision; one may not have that degree of ecstasy, but one can have experiences that are tremendously exciting. And in painting, too, there are moments when I see a tint in the sky or in nature and I try to get it onto paper and it seems to work, and I get a feeling of great excitement — all these experiences are, I think, related in some way to what the mystic must feel. There's something in human nature that manifests itself in all sorts of fields.

Yes.

I think there's a certain danger of stereotyping here; you feel, "Now that was an ecstatic experience", or "For me ecstasy is this type of experience", so that one becomes obsessed with a single model. But then you may suddenly realise that it's the moments when you have really "lived in the now*", as it were, that really matter, when you find that this experience is quite different from what one thought it was.*

Yes.

And your excitement and enthusiasm about nature, even if, as you say, you haven't felt the real "nature ecstasy", may help other people to have ecstatic feelings of their own; when you describe things you heighten my own awareness tremendously.

Well, what is enthusiasm but "the god within"? It is the divine flame. Then I always like to recall what Burke said: "It is enthusiasm that moves the world — but what a pity it is that all enthusiasts are liars!" It is enthusiasm that carries the politicians forward; it was enthusiasm that drove Hitler on.

Perhaps also one should remember that "entheos" in classical times referred to alcohol, the gift of the god Dionysus to man; when one drank it one had "the god within".

But then James calls alcohol "the poor man's mysticism". I think this is very true. In a way it's all the same experience, and I don't think alcohol is to be despised.

In education, too, despite all our wrong ideas there are times when a teacher's enthusiasm breaks through and a kind of "moment of feeling" results. But I think it's healthy to have Burke's comment quoted alongside; one can so easily get carried away by one's own supposed "charisma". One hesitates to ask for criteria when listening to someone sharing with you his dearest hopes and aspirations, but on the other hand one knows what may result when people get carried away by an uncritical enthusiasm.

I suppose one can't afford really to go to either extreme. You can't be all enthusiasm or be always demanding criteria. You've got to have the two sides balancing each other.

Perhaps we're back here to that division of labour; there are those who enthusiasm is valuable, so you encourage it, and others whose cold commonsense is valuable, so you encourage them too. Both the creative artist and the critic are needed in society.

Except that I sometimes have a feeling that we aren't going to be able to go on dividing up any longer.

I only suggest this is what does happen, not what should happen.

Yes, but it has become so destructive, when one kind of person isn't able to understand the other kind. If we're going to survive at all, we've all got to be able to do a bit of both. We must all do a bit of transcendence, and even the most transcendent have got to be a bit earthy.

One can't, of course, ask for specific means of achieving this kind of balance; but, with reference to education, would you say that there were particular vehicles, particular ways of developing this kind of awareness?

As far as children and young people are concerned, I would rather see it all done in terms of human relationships, — relationships with people for whom transcendent experience is normal.

What about the need to experience solitude?

I would myself take that need for granted, but I must say that my own children aren't at all interested in experiencing solitude as far as I can see. And perhaps if you haven't experienced solitude in early childhood you may be just unable to experience it later; I'm not sure. But you can't set that up. It's very important that one doesn't lay down standards about what it is OK for people to do, because in the end people can only do what they can do.

You say one can't lay down standards as to what they should do, but also one can't abdicate the responsibility of trying to help them.

Well in the end it isn't helpful to tell people they ought to be able to experience things that they can't experience; all you can do is inch along a fraction at a time to what you feel would be the happiest state of affairs. One gets such a feeling of inferiority if one is told that this is something everybody experiences and you aren't experiencing it yourself.

I'm just trying to feel for some kind of middle way between laying down standards in an authoritarian way and leaving people totally alone to make their own decisions without any kind of help — a state of affairs which some people seem to regard as ideal.

Yes, but you can't lay down standards any longer; all you can try to do is to be what you are and hope this comes in handy to others in some way. One can only see other people experiencing things and trying to express their experience, and this somehow gives one that little bit of strength to go on and try to experience things for oneself. This is certainly true of grown-ups. I don't know how far it is true of children.

I think it can help towards freedom if people can help you to look at your unconscious assumptions about life and society and your relationships with other people. I mean the sudden feeling you get, "My goodness I must always have always thought that without realising it, and I needn't think like that."

But one tends to discover that rather by observation than by what other people say. It's the things that other people have taken for granted, not what they have said, that have really given me a shock.

Monica Furlong

I think though that I've had this experience with one or two good teachers, who have, even in a quite intellectual way, been able to give me a sense of freedom.

Perhaps one of the things we don't any longer understand is the idea of apprenticeship or discipleship. If I try to think of anything in our society which in any way resembles this the only thing I can think of is in psychoanalysis; I mean the relationship which exists between analyst and analysand.

Casals I believe used to refuse to take pupils, but said people could just come and play with him.

Yes, this is a sort of discipleship isn't it?

And when Pissarro came to France and went to Corot and said, "Can I come and have lessons from you?" Corot said, "No, but you can come and work in my studio". The relationship there was a very interesting one; there was something in the old man's way of experiencing the world (his style) that the young man felt he could use to help express his own experience. Pissarro's very earliest pictures are a very moving tribute to his master. Buber's idea that the teacher should basically be a master is very alien to most of our present day educational writers.

One can think of very few people of whom one would say it was true. I think the idea is still valid, and perhaps when we have got over some of our anxieties about authority we shall come through to a state when we can once again experience authority without feeling so threatened by it. But then there are very few people in our society who actually have authority. Perhaps this is because we have despised and degraded old age.

This relationship of apprenticeship is like the one we were discussing earlier on; I mean the feeling of identification, when people feel they can identify with someone else and share his experience, can experience through him in some way. When a person has authority, he is a person whose experience you feel you can make your own.

Yes; but you've got to trust him, and be confident (a) that he really understands what he's on about and (b) that he's sufficiently humble and isn't going to take advantage of that authority.

7

Kallistos Ware

As with all forms of research, a great deal depends on the questions the investigator himself brings to his work, the problems that he himself would most like to see solved, or at any rate illuminated. Given the range of material at our disposal, could I ask where you would start?

I would begin by asking: What does this material tell me about the inward resources and potentialities of man? How far does it suggest that man can experience and know things in ways not normally allowed for? How far does it indicate that there are ways of understanding apart from those based on sense-perception and the reasoning of the conscious mind?

Of understanding what? The nature of man? Of reality? Of God?

That is the problem. You have collected data on the experiences that people actually have; but can you prove anything from these experiences alone, unless you have also certain outside standards or criteria by which you are going to interpret the experiences? I'm not clear whether you can get your criteria simply from the experiences themselves.

But in scientific research of other kinds, does one need to start with very clearly defined presuppositions?

Surely the scientific enquirer usually comes to his evidence with certain specific questions in his mind, which lead him to be looking for one thing rather than another. I am not sure, in the case of your group, what your questions are. Can the evidence prove anything unless you have questions to ask of it?

Our work at present is largely explanatory. We are exploring certain experiences of man, like men exploring plankton in the sea and first collecting specimens of it. Our first stage has been to ask people to send in accounts of their experiences, and we see the sort of range, from the sensory or the quasi-sensory through the telepathic and psychic to various other types of experience. That is what we are doing first. We get a certain amount of material that may not be very relevant — accounts of flying saucers and so on; we put them on one side. But out of all this there are certain sections that I hope will throw light on man's experience of the transcendental element, whether they call it God or not. There is such a thing as pure curiosity, isn't there?

Yes; but whether you prove much by pure curiosity I'm not sure.

Would you say that we are not really able to exercise curiosity about these things in any constructive way, without in some way letting our approach to them be affected by our own preconceptions?

My own starting-point, in approaching the material, would be rather different from yours. I start from the other end. I have been brought up within the framework of institutional religion, and while I have certainly been led to question that framework, I have never fundamentally rejected it. For me the important thing is that within that framework I should also have *personal experience*; that it shouldn't be merely a question of formal adherence to a particular set of beliefs, of the outward observance of particular religious practices, but that there should be a living, personal contact with the reality that is expressed communicated (albeit incompletely) through these beliefs and communicated by these practices. I am therefore interested in your material as evidence of the personal experience which others have had, but I naturally interpret that experience within the context of a Tradition that I accept and am trying to live. You, at any rate for the purposes of your inquiry, are starting from the other end. You are starting with the experience, without any kind of framework.

I don't think that anybody, whatever he may himself think, starts without presuppositions. We all no doubt have our own, which probably would be seen to differ considerably if we made them explicit one to another. But, given your presuppositions, what would you make of this body of material which we have? Your attitude seems at the moment to have some resemblance to that of the Moslem general who gave orders for the burning of the great library at Alexandria, on the grounds that if these writings were in accordance with the revelation of Allah to the Prophet they were unnecessary, and if they were contrary to it they were wicked. Would you feel the same towards a collection of accounts of religious experience? Would you think it was unnecessary, or of no interest?

Not at all: all first-hand experience is surely valuable, and can serve to illuminate the faith one already holds. Some of the questions I would want to ask are these. What connection do these experiences have with traditional religion? How far do they arise out of what people may have been taught about religion before they had them? How far have these experiences led people to alter their way of life, or to adopt any particular beliefs about God? If I had the chance to question the people who sent the accounts, these are the kind of things I would want to ask them. I would not want to treat each experience as something isolated, but to ask what is its context in relation to the entire life and beliefs of that person. This would interest me very much indeed.

Now you suggested that you were ready to discard some accounts as not relevant or not interesting. On what basis do you discard? Relevant to what?

Well, there are some that are of a purely psychic nature and not really religious at all, though there are some that are psychic and also have religious connections. I started this inquiry from the position of the biological humanist. I want to collect a body of evidence that will make people take seriously the idea that here is something in man's make-up that is obviously very real to him. Now you implied that some of the experiences would be closer to institutional religion than others, in terms of their effect, and that you would be interested, so to speak, to space them out in this respect.

Yes. I certainly do not mean that I judge the value of the experiences solely in terms of whether they bring a person closer to instituional religion or not; but nonetheless that does seem to me relevant — perhaps more as shedding light on the nature of organized religion than as illuminating the experiences in themselves.

What do you feel about the sort of conclusion that William James draws that, in relation to many experiences, the belief, the theological formulation that lies behind them, is more or less irrelevant? Would you be disconcerted if you felt this to be so?

For me the ultimate interest in any account of religious experience depends on the degree to which the experience points beyond itself, towards some greater reality, transcendent or immanent. I do not wish to treat the experience only as a psychological entity, isolated on its own, but I wish to treat it also as (potentially, at any rate,) an account of something else. Of course I do not expect the accounts to "prove" theological formulations in any direct way; but I do hope that they might deepen my understanding of the formulations. If the experiences proved to be totally irrelevant — yes, I should be disconcerted.

There is another point that I should add. Any statement in human language about God or religious experience is inevitably inadequate; not necessarily untrue, but inadequate. You cannot express these things properly in human language, first because language is not sufficiently adapted to express them, and secondly because the human mind does not understand enough about God; and therefore no religious truth can be fully and completely contained in a dogma. A dogma is only a signpost, and I am prepared to accept that you can have more than one kind of signpost. So I am not expecting your material to confirm one particular type of verbal formulation, and to refute all the others.

But you do have criteria by which you can decide that one way of talking is more adequate than another, don't you? Could you say what they are?

My primary criterion would be that of personal encounter, because I believe that God is personal. I do not mean by this that God is a person in exactly the same sense in which we sitting in this room are persons; but that if we are going to talk about God we are brought closest to the truth by thinking of Him as personal, by thinking of our relation to God as parallel to our relation to each other as persons. I should therefore be concerned to discover how far the accounts of religious experience, without necessarily using the word "person", yet seem to imply some idea of meeting a greater reality in a personal way. I would be less interested in experiences which express a diffused nature-mysticism, which express, say, a feeling of the wonder and the beauty of the world around us; as when a man looks at a tree and suddenly exclaims, "There is a great marvel in this tree". Certainly I consider such experiences important, but ultimately less significant. I would wish, above all, to concentrate on those experiences which imply contact with a reality filling the whole world and yet greater than the whole world, and which express some feeling that our encounter with this reality is not just an experience of impersonal power but is in some sense a personal meeting similar to that which human beings have with each other. This would be the first criterion that I would apply.

But some meetings between human beings are more personal than others. What is it that distinguishes an encounter or a meeting that is truly personal?

To me the idea of knowing a person is very closely linked with the idea of love for a person. Unless we have some relationship of love towards others, we do not really know them but merely know facts about them, which is not at all the same thing. Therefore I am interested to find out: Do these accounts of religious experience manifest in some way an awareness that this greater reality — around them and in them — in some sense loves them, and that they are called to love it in return? That would be my primary test to establish whether an experience is genuinely personal.

I can think of at least one case where there was a strong impression of love given in very impersonal terms, where someone speaks of a constant conviction of a force for goodness and for love lying behind everything. There is a stress on the immanent aspect, although attached to the idea of love, without any awareness of the transcendence which I imagine you would find in any personal encounter.

Love would not necessarily imply transcendence. However, when we meet other people, we are aware of that other person being external to us. No, "external" is not the right word; when we achieve a loving relationship with others, we are united to them, yet it is a union without confusion. The "I" and the "Thou" meet but do not annihilate each other; we are conscious of the "Thou" as being *other.*

I am certainly interested in people who express this conviction of a very diffuse power for goodness, a sense of the absolute which they think of as loving and good. How do they come to think of this force in such diffuse immanent terms, and yet having goodness attached to it? Would you say that, without the personal element, this is rather a powerless concept? And that some element of the transcendent is necessary here?

I am not happy about too sharp a contrast between immanence and transcendence. Could you have an experience that there was something that loved you and that you could love, without also having the experience that this power had in it some kind of purpose and direction — to use our human language, some kind of will? Does your material shed light on this?

There are people who have described their experience in these terms, but it may be that the accounts which we have are not adequate. But may I come back to this question of presuppositions? You have told us what criteria you would apply to these accounts of experience. These criteria are themselves based upon your own experience?

Yes.

Would you expect them to be convincing to people who had not had that experience? Other people might say, "My criteria are quite different; I am approaching this material from a phenomenological point of view. As for this idea of a transcendent power, well, other people may speak of it but I myself have had no experiences of it. I am merely interested in these particular phenomena because they seem to me to be most curious." How would you approach people who took that line, people who had quite different presuppositions from your own — presuppositions which they may regard as equally valid? Why should one not for example take what appears to be a more scientific attitude to these phenomena, and regard them purely as phenomena, without reading too much purpose into them? Some people might say that this is what you are doing.

Could an atheist in fact do our work?

Up to a point I'm sure he could. But if you dispense with all presuppositions, in what sense are you undertaking research into religious experience, and not just into human experience as such?

I think one must say that nobody approaches a scientific problem without having a certain hunch, a certain hypothesis; and I have a hypothesis which I think has a biological basis. My belief in a personal God, one who can be approached with devotion and love, has a biological basis. You see, I think something's happened in biology. There is something very similar to man's relationship to God in the relationship of the dog to man. Here we have a most extraordinary thing that has actually taken place: the dog has switched his allegiance from his ordinary pack-leader to quite a new master — man. And man by breeding has preserved a lot of the more infantile characters of the dog, including his motherly affection which again is transferred on to the new master. And so you've got an animal that is loyal to a new master, and has a love and devotion to him. Well, I think that when man began to realise that there was a power outside the self that he could approach in various ways, he began to personalize it. I think man is a creature that has become religious; just as the dog has become devoted to his master, we can have a love-relationship to this power beyond the self which we can only approach as if we were approaching a person. So I believe that religion has a deep biological basis.

And the world is *a very curious place. We came across, not so very long ago, a case of what* may *have been levitation. I should love to know if levitation really occurs, and under what circumstances. Need I have some justification for this curiosity?*

None at all. I welcome this approach. I would contrast it with the attitude of my former philosophy tutor who once said to me: "It seems to me that religion is trying to answer questions that can't be answered, and in any case I'm not interested in the questions." Naturally I disagree with both parts of this statement, but particularly with the second part. For there is surely enough evidence in the people and the world around us to indicate that he should, as an intelligent and open-minded person, at least be interested in the questions. What presumably he meant was that a view of the world that limited itself to the accepted methods of scientific inquiry and to the ordinary processes of discursive reason answered all the questions that he was interested in. I am sure that there are a great many questions which these methods and processes do not answer. As you say, people do have experiences of levitation, telepathy, being out of the body and so on, which suggest that there are ways of knowing and understanding markedly different from those that we normally employ. So it would certainly be important if you could establish, empirically, by scientific methods, the inadequacy of a view which restricts itself narrowly to the normal data of sense-perceptions, and if you could prove instead that the data are very much more varied.

Clearly there are many questions raised by so-called "abnormal" experiences. By what right, for example, do we say that when I am sitting in this room now and look around at you all, this is a real experience, but that when someone has an out-of-the-body experience it is unreal? In a sense they are both real; they both happen. And therefore they each equally require to be fitted into a wider framework, if possible. I see the need for a purely phenomenological and empirical approach. But as soon as you start classifying the material, it is difficult to avoid being influenced by presuppositions. You have said that you classify some experiences as psychic, and others as religious. What in fact do you mean — no doubt many others have asked you this question — by a "religious" experience? What quality in the experences reported to you entitles you to treat one experience as religious and another, say an experience of extra-sensory perception, as devoid of religious content?

Would it be unkind to ask you how you yourself would answer that question?

I can think of two methods of approach that I might adopt. One is to ask: how does this experience fit into the rest of this person's life? Sometimes, for example, people have a strong conviction that something is going to happen, and it happens exactly in that way; they just say "What an odd coincidence", and it doesn't make any difference to their life. At other times people have an experience such that they never forget it, and they feel that the experience has altered the whole direction of their life and has given them a new way of looking at the world. I would say that the second type of experience clearly has a religious quality (in the widest sense of the word "religious"), which the first lacks. That is one criterion: did the experience in question matter to that person, did it make a decisive difference to the quality of their life?

A problem arises, of course, when one has record of some such experience which may not yet have had any permanent influence on the person's life, though subsequently it may do so; or we may have an account of the event but not of its effect. We have to be very careful what we rule out.

Yes, I agree. Let me come to my second criterion. The subsequent effect of an experience on someone's life is what I would call an *external* criterion, in that it is outside the experience itself. What would I look for *inside* the experience? I spoke earlier of personality and love. A third characteristic that I would look for inside the experience is a sense of unity — a conviction that everything is fundamentally one and interconnected, that there is something joining all things together. I suppose this is a very frequent theme in accounts of mystical experience in almost all religious traditions. It is the feeling that St. Benedict had when he saw a ray of light and felt that within this ray of light he had seen the whole of creation. If a person spoke in that kind of way, I would wish to know more about his experience.

Could you say why you feel this to be so important?

Because one of the arguments that people give in favour of belief in God is that this belief enables them to see reality as a whole, in a way that nothing else does. And so I am very interested when people say that they have had an experience in which they saw everything as a whole, not in fragments but suddenly all together.

This might give rather more value in your eyes to the experience of the man who saw a great marvel in a tree. You didn't seem to be so interested in him before.

I agree: I should have taken him more seriously. At that point I was thinking merely of the heightened perception of an object. But such a heightened perception may very easily be linked with a conviction that in this particular object I am seeing and understanding everything; and if a person felt that, it would to me be much more interesting. One of the reasons why I have introduced this idea of all things as a unity is to avoid the immanent/transcendent dichotomy.

Do you think that this sense of unity can also evoke a sense of purposive direction?

Let me try to express my line of thought by making a distinction between the individual and the person. People who are isolated, lacking deep contact with others, are just units, individuals. You become a real person by having contact with others, by living in them and for them, by your sharing in their experience and by their sharing in yours. That is why I said that there can be no genuine knowledge of other people without love for them. The man who loves nobody, and lives simply within and for himself, is on the whole extremely uninteresting. Now when someone suddenly experiences the universe as a unity, this seems to be an extension of his experience of personal relations: instead of just feeling that he shares things with particular people who are his friends, he suddenly has the conviction that the entire universe is joined together by some such kind of sharing, that there is in this sense a unity. Such experiences of unity can in this way be regarded as experiences of a personal reality in the universe beyond that of the particular human persons whom we meet.

May I ask how one, speaking from within the Orthodox tradition, would describe the relationship between that type of experience which would normally be called psychic and that which might normally be called spiritual? I am thinking, for example, of the relationship between telepathy and prayer. How does the Orthodox tradition view these things?

In general there is a great reserve towards psychic phenomena. To give just one example, a writer of the 5th century, Diadochus of Photice, says: "Let no-one who hears us speak of the perceptive faculty of the intellect imagine that by this we mean that the glory of God appears to man visibly . . . If light or some fiery form should be seen by one pursuing the spiritual way, he should not on any account accept such a vision; it is an obvious deceit of the enemy. Many indeed have had this experience and in their ignorance have turned aside from the way of truth." (*Century* 36) This suggests that Diadochus was quite familiar with the fact that people who try to pray intensively will often experience psychic phenomena — odd things going on; and he considers that if they pay undue attention to these things then they will be wandering from the right path.

Generally speaking, within the Orthodox tradition we consider that "paranormal" experiences, that is, experiences that do not come to us though the normal use of our five senses, can be on three levels: they can be positively evil, diabolical; they can be from God; or they can be neutral — there are many forces in the world with which you can come into contact which are not necessarily directly from God or directly from the devil. The experiences originating from the devil are to be at once repelled; those from God are to be accepted; those that are neutral are to be ignored. How do you distinguish? The first rule is simply to take no notice and to continue praying; if they go away, then they are not important. Two other tests can also be applied. The first is external: What effect do these experiences have on your daily life? Do they make you a better person in your dealings with other people? If they do not, then this would be an indication that there is something wrong in these experiences. Here we have the old test of "by their fruits you will know them". The other is interior: if a thing is from God, it is absolutely convincing; it leaves no element of doubt in your mind that this is God, that now I am face to face with the true reality in the universe and beyond the universe. If there is doubt in your mind, then you should ignore the experience. If you can ignore it and forget about it, this again is generally an indication that it is not from God. When a true experience from God comes, it will have such power in it that it cannot be ignored. The basic inward criterion is summed up in the

Greek term *plerophoria,* meaning assurance, an overwhelming conviction.

But people who are utterly deluded also have this absolute assurance. What about devils disguised as angels of light?

Yes, the devil does disguise himself as an angel, but he is never entirely convincing; to the inward eye of one practised in *diakrisis,* "discernment" or "discrimination", there will be some jarring note that gives him away. But on many occasions it is extremely difficult to distinguish rightly. There is no test which, applied mechanically, can by itself automatically supply the right answer. But if someone is sincerely pursuing the spiritual way, then gradually — through prayer, study, fasting, obedience and active service to others — he will develop a spiritual "taste" which directly and intuitively enables him to distinguish the genuine or divine from the counterfeit or demonic, just as our natural taste enables us immediately to distinguish wholesome food from food that has gone mouldy. But the dangers of delusion remain very great. So the safest rule, especially at the initial stages of the spiritual life, is to say: Take no notice of the sounds, shapes or lights; simply persevere in the work of prayer.

Another test or criterion should be mentioned. Anybody seriously seeking to practice inward prayer, whether he is a monk or a lay person, will seek out an "elder", a spiritual guide or *starets,* someone more experienced than himself, to whom the person will disclose his experiences and thoughts, even when he himself does not think they are specially remarkable. If someone had a vision, for example, he would at once submit it to the judgement of his *starets.* Of course, this criterion is not infallible. The *starets* may say he has no advice to give, or may himself be deceived.

If a person has an experience which you on investigation perceive to be of a demonic influence disguised as an angel of light, would you say that this experience had been a delusion?

Yes, I would say that it was a delusion — a delusion which has from one point of view failed, since it has been recognized for what it is. I don't want to suggest that immediate, "paranormal" experiences of demonic power are at all frequent in the Orthodox tradition. I simply mention that as one possibility. Far more usually the reaction of a spiritual director when presented with "paranormal" experiences would be, "This is probably a fantasy of your own that results from the fact that you are not eating or sleeping enough; and therefore let us say no more about it." If the person accepts this explanation, that already shows that the experience does not have an intensely compelling and self-authenticating character. When it is so definite that the person replies, "You only say that because you didn't have the experience; I know it was something outside me, it wasn't just fantasy or imagination", then the spiritual director might need to look at it further.

I think there is a certain potential danger in this criterion of assurance; it is after all only assurance for those who have it. And we are all familiar, both in educational circles and beyond, with certain types of Christians who are so dead assured of their own salvation that they think the same recipe is compulsory for everybody else.

I agree that there are very great dangers. It is impossible to devise rules which you can apply universally and which will infallibly give you an answer. I only suggest these rules as one way of sifting things.

I have an idea that those who have a passion to know the nature of truth, of the good, are more likely to be rewarded with religious experience. Perhaps the orientation of the person concerned is important?

I agree; you cannot isolate the experience as something on its own; it has to be seen in relation to the person's whole character and attitude to life.

I think there is another danger in taking whether or not a person is convinced of the reality of his experience as a criterion for its being genuine. The more convinced a person is, the more difficult it is for him to go back and know something about the circumstances of his original experience; I think he is bound to build on it, and to reinterpret it in the light of his subsequent experience. And so when he describes his original experience, you are not therefore necessarily getting a correct account of it; you are seeing a picture of his subsequent life. The more convinced a person is of the reality of his experience, the more likely he is to do this. Would you agree that this is a problem?

Yes, that does seem to be a problem. Within the context of spiritual direction in the Orthodox Church, a person would be urged to inform his *starets* at once — if possible, to go and see him that very hour; and in a normal monastic setting, probably he could do this. Naturally you are working in a different situation. If someone came to me long afterwards and told me about some experience, I would inquire about his life subsequent to the experience. Did the experience alter his life? If it did not, I would find it less interesting; it would be something quite unrelated to anything else. But indeed one runs the risk of subsequent reinterpretation.

Some people write very vividly of an experience and end up by saying that it has not had the slightest effect on their subsequent way of life. Perhaps these accounts of experience are the more reliable ones?

I suppose they might be. But may I raise a slightly different point? No doubt in your inquiries you find it necessary to distinguish between experience and experiences. From the nature of the case I imagine that most of the evidence you have is of experiences, of particular incidents. But there must also be many people who consider that they have religious experience in a wider sense, as something which extends through their whole life, though they could not point to any special moment when they had any extraordinary experience of which they could send you a description. This seems to be relevant to the problem raised just now: you might have a person who has had an experience in the narrower sense, and this may have affected his total attitude to life — his total experience in the wider sense; this total experience will then react on his interpretation of that original single experience.

Yes, it is this total attitude that is really much more important than any single experience, however dramatic or impressive. What matters is the growth of what might be called spiritual awareness.

I am glad that you say this. If I told a member of my own parish, "Here is this institute investigating religious experience, why don't you write in to them?" he would probably say, "But I have nothing that would interest them, nothing remarkable or exceptional." But if I then said to him, "But surely you have religious experience, surely your religion is not just a formal profession of faith, a mechanical performance of ritual; do you not feel that you know God personally?" he would (I hope) say "yes". However, he might find it extremely difficult to put this down in the form of a report to someone else.

In fact both these types of experience are well represented in our records. But would you not perhaps say that for some people it might be quite wholesome for them to try to put into words the experience they have had, might it not reveal to them something about themselves? It is so often assumed that experience of the supernatural, the transcendent, or whatever one chooses to call it, is beyond words. Yet when one tries to describe it one may surprise oneself. Some of our writers seem to have found this.

Yes: when we are deeply moved by an experience, we often find in ourselves unexpected powers of description. The transcendent, in the strict sense, is indeed beyond words; but we can provide verbal "pointers" — often very effective "pointers".

May I go back to the question of your presuppositions? There are three things you haven't mentioned, and I wonder how important you would think they are. Firstly, if it is true that this personal, loving reality does demand love for other human beings, to what extent would you agree that there is a demand in all religious experience? Secondly, how far is there a demand that one should be a member of a community of worshippers? And thirdly, there is a recurring note in all Christian writing that this "other reality" is vulnerable, is crucifiable for example, and that it is integral to its reality that one can, in fact, wound it.

Your first point is whether this reality makes demands on one in regard to one's relations with other people. Certainly I consider this a criterion. If you are using a purely phenomenological approach perhaps it is dangerous to speak of true or false experience; experience is experience, and to talk of true or false is to pass a value judgement. I, on my side, am prepared to pass such a value judgement; and a primary criterion which would guide me in doing so is precisely the point which you mention, that this reality makes demands that we should love others; and if we do not respond to those demands then one of two things probably follows: either there was something wrong in the experience itself, and it was not a genuine experience of God; or else it was indeed a true experience, but we, for our part, proved false to it. So I accept your first point, and I see it implied in the test I mentioned earlier, "by their fruits you shall know them". One way of testing the value of an experience is to consider its effect on a man's life, precisely in the field of his personal relations with others.

But I was concentrating not on whether it had an effect, but on whether he felt that it ought to.

Certainly I consider that he should feel this. I am using the word "should", conscious that I am passing a value judgement, and that in a purely empirical approach you do not say "should" or "ought" of an experience; it's just there.

Your second point is about membership of a community. Within the Orthodox tradition, it is assumed that someone pursuing the spiritual way is sharing in the corporate life of the Church — participating in liturgical worship, regularly receiving Holy Communion, going to confession, consulting his *starets*, reading the Bible daily, and so on. So if he has an unusual experience, he would ask himself: "How does this fit into the framework of my membership in the Church's corporate life?" And if it doesn't seem to fit, this would make him suspicious of the experience, though he wouldn't necessarily reject it at once. I accept, however, that genuinely religious experiences may happen to people who do not belong to any religious community; and I wouldn't expect that the experience, in itself, contained explicitly some command to join a church body. But perhaps subsequently, in trying to live up to the experience, the person might find that he could not do so in isolation.

Your third point is whether the reality is vulnerable. Yes, I believe that it is. To me this is implied in the idea of love. Is not love in its essence vulnerable? Love implies openness. If somebody loves you, that means they are affected by what you do and they can be hurt by it. If nothing you do can cause them anguish, in what sense do they love you? This is speaking on the level of human beings. But I am willing to apply this to God as well, while making proper allowances for the apophatic approach.

Some people who have written to us have said that they could not find in the Christian church an acceptance of their deepest experiences, so that they were driven out of the church rather than brought into it. What sort of place do you see individual experience as having in the total reality of the Christian tradition? Do you feel that the church may have undervalued individual experience?

Our aim, as we advance upon the spiritual way, is to gain experience (in the singular), that is, total spiritual awareness. We are not to seek experiences (in the plural) as an end in themselves, still less should we try to induce them through our own efforts; that would be to encourage a kind of emotionalism or religious hedonism. But at the same time we ought to impress on people that Christianity is not just a question of ritual, moral rules, and abstract adherence to verbal doctrinal formulations; each is called to relive the Tradition in his own personal experience. We should tell people that remarkable experiences do happen, and that, while they may be a delusion from the devil, they may be a gift from God. We should, however, always be seeking not God's gifts but God Himself. The experiences are important, not in isolation, but because they may point beyond themselves to Him.

Would you agree that in the whole history of religion its impetus has been the desire to understand life, to respond appropriately to life, and that an essential quality of any experience that can be called religious is that it is one that in some sense leads to integration, a more integrated response to life?

Yes, one of the qualities in an experience which would lead me to call it religious is that it is creative, that it is life-enhancing. This is only another way of what was said earlier, that such an experience makes a difference to people's lives; it makes them in some sense deeper and more meaningful as persons, giving them a power which they could not have otherwise.

Could it perhaps be said that the traditional church is not in fact integrated, in that it does not function on the level of the whole of people's experience? To how many priests, for example, could you go and say you had had a very significant dream?

There is an ever-present danger of reducing religion to a philosophical theory or a moral code; whereas the primary purpose of the Church on earth is to bring people, through prayer, to a direct apprehension of the living God. Of course such an apprehension should then transform our personal relations to others and inspire us to serve them in a new way. But if in our religious teaching we speak only of service to others, divorced from the direct apprehension of God through prayer, then we reduce the Church to a kind of welfare organization. I sympathize with your emphasis upon the *whole* of people's experience. Certainly, when I participate in the Orthodox Liturgy, I have the sense that this is not just a public meeting but that with the whole of myself I am being taken up into an invisible action greater than myself, greater than the visible congregation. Public worship should not appeal solely to the reasoning brain or the will or the emotions, but should help to activate within us what we called earlier a *total* spiritual awareness. I think the churches have often failed here; but perhaps more in the West than in the Christian East.

Most Orthodox spiritual fathers whom I have known take a serious interest in people's dreams, while emphasizing the need for sobriety and the dangers of fantasy. Dreams are one of the ways in which we experience things important for our life, one of the ways in which God speaks to us. Of course a dream may come not from God but from the devil or from our natural physical or psychic processes. But it may possess genuine spiritual value.

I suppose one side-effect of a piece of research such as that being done by this Unit is that it might help to enlarge the Church's sympathies, its criteria of what it will look at or consider relevant.

I hope it will do so, and such a service could be of the utmost value to the Church. In this connection I remember a remark made by the Serbian Bishop Nicolai of Zicha, who said: "A faith without miracles is just a philosophical system, and a church without miracles is just a philanthropic society like the Red Cross." I am sure he didn't mean that philosophy or the Red Cross is unnecessary, but simply that the Church should offer something more; and by "miracles" he meant one aspect of what we refer to as direct religious experience. What is a miracle? It is, basically, something that surpasses the normal ways in which we know, the normal ways in which things happen. Probably you in this Unit prefer not to talk about "miracles" in your inquiry because the word implies too many presuppositions. But if through your inquiries, carried out according to strictly scientific methods, you can help to establish that man is capable of experiences traditionally labelled "mystical" or "miraculous", then we in the Church should be profoundly grateful to you. You will be broadening our understanding of what man is.

8

Carmen Blacker, Freda Wint

Buddhism is commonly regarded as an atheistic religion. How far would you say this was true?

F.W. That's a very complicated question. Buddhists believe in the transcendence. If they didn't, I don't think we could call Buddhism a religion. The difficulty is in trying to explain expressions like this. There is a story about a King of Siam who had to face this problem rather unexpectedly. His name was Mongkut, and he was a contemporary of Queen Victoria. He had spent thirty-two years as a monk, a Buddhist bhikkhu; he was in hiding from a relative who was then on the throne. When his relative died, he succeeded to the throne, and he reformed the Buddhist Order in Siam — quite magnificently, but that's another story. Then he received a letter from Queen Victoria, addressed to him as a brother monarch, and he was faced with the problem of replying to her in proper form. He replied in English, and composed the letter himself since he was the most proficient English scholar in Siam. (His letter is in the Bodleian, incidentally). Queen Victoria had written to him: "From Victoria, by the Grace of God Queen of England, Empress of India" and all her other titles. King Mongkut pondered over his reply, and finally decided to write: "From Mongkut, by the Grace of the Chief Super-agency of the Universe, King of Siam." It was a crux of theology, and of tact.

How was that?

F.W. Well, the nub of the problem is that in early Buddhism, God, conceived as a person, is part of the world, the universe, including of course the universe of spiritual beings, and so he would be liable to the vicissitudes of life, and especially change, impermanence. The transcendence for Buddhists is outside all the spheres of gods, spirits, human beings, animals and so on. But King Mongkut was a learned man and he knew that Christians see their God as being also, by nature the transcendence — which is a whole other way of looking at it, and a non-concept for a Buddhist brought up in the early tradition. So he avoided the term "God", but courteously, and I think rather charmingly. Ceylonese Buddhists, on the other hand, are much more uncompromisingly atheistic in tone, partly for historical reasons.

Why is this so?

F.W. The Ceylonese suffered a lot of cruelty at the hands of Christians from Europe from the sixteenth century onwards, and later on, in the nineteenth century, when Europeans had become less generally cruel, at least locally in Ceylon, Christianity was still the religion of the imperialist power. Siam managed to avoid an imperialist take-over, so relations were much easier. One of King Mongkut's personal friends was the Catholic Bishop Pallegoix, for instance. But, to return to the point — atheism — if you look at the early Buddhist scriptures there is a great deal of discussion about the nature of Brahma, which is the Pali name for God. The chief attribute of Brahma, in the Pali Canon, is love. When a human being develops the virtue of loving kindness, his heart has become a temple of Brahma, they say: and the Buddhist way is called the "Brahma-faring". Coming as I do from a Christian culture, I am drawn to passages of this kind; I find them heart-warming.

Does this apply to Japanese Buddhism too?

C.B. I think in the Mahayana, the Buddha is a god. You have to differentiate between the popular religion, where nearly always you find some object of worship, and the more scholarly circles of the monastery. But the Mahayana itself is divided into various sects which are very different from each other. Take for instance the ones which worship Amida. Amida really functions like a god. He's a saviour, the agent by which you can achieve your salvation (and this is surely one of the things a god does for you?); it's by his grace that you are guided to the Pure Land on death, and in the Pure Land you can be sure of ultimately attaining Nirvana. He's treated in the temples as a god. If you take the Tantric sect, the main Buddha worshipped is Vairochara, and again, he's treated like a god. There the aim of meditation is to become one with him, by a number of mudras of the hand and mantras and visualizations. You have to become one with the Buddha. We haven't quite decided what a god is, but isn't he, in one of his aspects, an object of worship by whose grace you can achieve salvation? And surely salvation is what any religious person is aiming at, isn't it? We feel there's something wrong with us at present, and we're aiming at a state of wholeness and perfection which we call salvation.

It would be true to say, wouldn't it, that much of the vogue certainly of Zen Buddhism in the West is due to the fact that it presents a kind of abstract alternative to the more personal religious traditions we have known.

C.B. Perhaps; but I don't know what the attraction is of the thing that many people in the West call Zen, because it doesn't seem to bear any relationship to what I know as Zen in Japan.

I mean the kind of Zen one might get from people like Alan Watts.

C.B. I think that's utter rubbish. Enlightenment is according to him simply a matter of "letting go", without any preliminary discipline.

F.W. It's all this freedom and liberation, and self-expression: let go and throw over all the rules. Enlightenment has been reduced to throwing over the moral law.

What about Suzuki's presentation of Zen?

C.B. The trouble about Dr. Suzuki's writings is that he didn't understand how ignorant western people could be. He concentrated on the enlightenment experience without bothering to write much about the struggles needed to get to that stage. What you have to ask about Zen writings is, when did people make a particular statement? If somebody says there's nothing to do and nowhere to go, you must ask, in what point in their career did they say this. Did they say it after thirty years' hard struggle, or did they say it before they had started struggling? I think you'll usually find they said it on the other side of the river. In which case the meaning of the words is entirely different from what it would be if they were said before they set out at all. For somebody at the beginning of the Path to say there's nothing to do and nowhere to go — this just doesn't make sense. You know the parable about the raft going across the river, which I think is so vivid: once you're on the other side of the river you look back and it seems as though the river's disappeared; it isn't there at all.

How does the parable go?

C.B. You think there's a river in front of you and you think you need a vehicle to take you across. You are quite convinced you are crossing a river, until you reach the other side and look back, and both the river and the raft have disappeared. Nevertheless you needed the raft to take you across.

I still don't quite see what it means.

F.W. Perhaps because this parable is a famous Mahayana paradox. In the early texts, the Buddha is quoted as saying that the teaching is a raft; you use it to cross the river but when you get to the other bank, you don't cart it around on your head. But it's interesting to see how the concept has changed. I was talking about "God", and you started talking about "a god". I was thinking more in terms of "God" as the monotheistic religions understand the word, and you were talking about gods more in the sense of the devas.

C.B. I was talking rather about somebody who is worshipped as a sacred object. I do think it is necessary to draw a distinction between sacred and profane here. If you're thinking in religious terms at all, you have to think that there's a barrier between the two realms. The universe is not simply in one dimension; it's not all within our competence. I think this is what I object to so much about humanists: they seem to think that the whole universe is potentially within the competence of man. I don't think it is: there's a barrier, beyond which the sacred lies. You need grace; you need to become what you are not now in order to understand. I think this is what religion is; a confrontation with the sacred. I would call God a power coming from the other side of the barrier, whom you could worship, who was helping you to achieve this perfection.

Very like the "grace" of Christianity.

C.B. Yes, but I think there's a tendency among some Buddhists to make the raft into a kind of technique. I don't like this: it makes it too mundane. It sounds as though it's just like learning to carve, or learning to cook. Still, there is something you can learn to do for yourself. Yes, the raft is like grace, except that you have to co-operate.

Perhaps the raft is grace, and we have to provide the oars. And the raft could be not only Zen or any specifically Buddhist teaching, but any religious tradition that is appropriate to the individual concerned. Hence the great variety of rafts, all of which must in the end be discarded when we reach that state of grace.

C.B. Yes; and one may take another metaphor, that of Yoga in its proper sense; that which yokes you to the divine, yet something which you yourself can do. But it's not a technique such that if you do this and this then inevitably the result will be enlightenment. It's not like that. There's so much more to take into consideration: your own Karma, and the causes that have brought you to your present state. What will take one man on to a state of enlightenment may well not work with another man.

Are you saying that the nearest analogy is some kind of personal relatedness, so that what you are doing for yourself is also a kind of response?

C.B. Yes, I think so. Wouldn't you say so, Freda? Or is there no personal response from the other side?

F.W. *Personal* response? It's the word "personal" that I find difficult.

It's a difficult concept to convey without using the word "personal" simply because "grace" has this suggestion of help, as something active or dynamic which comes out to meet you as you make your move towards it. So your experience is more like some sort of personal inter-relatedness than anything else.

F.W. I do find this question difficult because, in as much as there is a concept of "grace" in Buddhism, it lies in the fact that the teaching has been brought into the world, and that is not exactly a personal thing. There is no feeling in the Theravada, I think, of a *personal* God. I find that it is more like the Absolute which one is endeavouring to discover in one's own life. But I agree with Carmen that one has to make the link with the transcendence, and all Buddhists believe that our minds have the potentiality for doing this. Perhaps that's "grace" too.

C.B. Yes, you simply cannot generalize about these things. Take the sects of the Mahayana which worship Amida: they rely completely on grace: there is nothing I can do, they would say, because I am fundamentally wrong. It's entirely by the grace of Amida that anything can be done towards my salvation. You have completely different schools on the subject of grace.

F.W. And you find this, I suppose, in Christianity too. There's a very strong devotional element in some branches. Elsewhere, for example in Eckhardt, one almost loses this sense of the personal. There seem to be two distinct streams in human temperament. Some people like the devotional, the personal: that's their way; whereas for others the more abstract is the more natural way.

C.B. Yes, some people want to feel that there's something they can do for themselves. Just to sit back and wait for grace is very difficult for them.

Would you say that the Amida form of Buddhism is like the Bhakti way in Hinduism?

C.B. Yes, very much so; the idea of devotion is very strong in both of them.

Do they both have the same idea of incarnation?

C.B. Well, Amida is supposed to have been, aeons and aeons ago, a monk who made 48 vows that, if he became a Buddha, he would save all sentient beings that called on his name. There are a whole series of these vows, and the eighteenth states that anyone who calls on his name with true and perfect faith will be born into the "Pure Land". The Pure Land is one of the paradises — there are lyrical descriptions in the appropriate Sutras — where strictly, under ideal conditions, you can be sure of attaining Nirvana. But most people don't bother about that: Paradise is quite good enough for them to pass the rest of eternity in. But again there's nothing in this life that you can do. Even the calling on Amida's name in true faith is a grace. There was a priest in Japan in the 13th century called Shinran who carried this doctrine to the absolute limit. He reminds one slightly of St. Augustine, though he was a good deal more merciful. There's absolutely nothing that I can do; I may think that I am calling with true faith, but in fact I am not; I simply have to wait for grace to help me.

F.W. Whereas early Buddhists were Pelagian.

C.B. Yes, I suppose so.

And which do you belong to?

F.W. Early Buddhism: I'm a Pelagian.

C.B. But then there are other Mahayana sects, one in Japan for example called *jiriki* which means "self-help", (as opposed to *tariki* which means "other-help"). Zen is very much of the *jiriki* type: there you have to struggle with your meditation and discipline.

Is the Tantric tradition closer to the Theravada or the Pure Land?

C.B. It's Mahayana, but not at all near the Pure Land — except that Amida is one of five Buddhas in the Tantric Pantheon; but the doctrine is quite different.

You said that your kind of Buddhism was Pelagian; but you did say that the Dharma was given.

F.W. But didn't Pelagius also say that the way in which God helps man is first of all through the teaching given by Jesus?

Well, yes; Pelagius himself has been greatly misunderstood. We tend to use the word "Pelagian" to mean that man can get by on his own; but he himself admitted that fundamentally in the whole universe there is this element of the given without which we'd be sunk.

F.W. But he wouldn't ever have gone as far as Augustine who said to God: "Demand of me any virtue you like, but give me the virtue you demand." It was at this point when the Confessions were being read aloud in Rome that Pelagius got up and left the room.

C.B. Weren't there some people called "Semi-Pelagian"?

F.W. What Buddhists really don't hold with is the idea of the creator God. This is the real issue. There's a light-hearted parable in Theravada Buddhism of the creator of this world finding himself as it were. One of the higher Devas fell out of the world of pure abstraction into a lower world of forms; and he became conscious in this world, and he was the only being in it. So he felt, "Here I am, the only being; I must be the first of beings". So he began to create; he created universes. Then another of the high Devas fell from the abstract realms to this lower world, and he saw this creator; and he said, you were here before me; you must be the Creator of All. So he bowed down to him. Then other Devas came, and this was the Pantheon, under this Deva, who in his delusion thought he was the creator of all. This is the Buddhist tale of how a minor creator god fell into a state of delusion; it emphasizes the Buddhist attitude to matter.

Am I right in thinking that the Buddha himself had no interest in these theological questions?

F.W. The "ten answered questions", yes. Basically they boil down to four. The first two are to do with speculations about the beginnings of the universe: the Buddha said that it was useless to speculate about that. He always believed in making empirical discoveries, rather than running on about unsubstantiated views. And another of the questions was what happens to the enlightened one after death. He put that aside because he said that the unenlightened mind wasn't capable of conceiving what does happen. And the fourth question was one about the nature of the soul.

Didn't he put these questions aside as likely to distract you from the ethics which he thought were more important?

F.W. Yes: ethics and meditation practice and struggle with the defilements of mind — all the things one should do, which too much metaphysical speculation could simply become a substitute for. There is a story of one man who refused to stay with the Buddha and go on any longer unless the Buddha would explain to him what was the origin of the universe. "In that case", said the Buddha, "you'd better be off."

C.B. Yes, he said he was like a man who has been pierced by a poisoned arrow, and whose first task obviously is to pull the arrow out, but who instead asks what was the name of the man who shot the arrow and what was his father's name and where does he live and where was he born, wasting time when the obvious thing to do is to pull the arrow out.

F.W. But the Unanswered Questions have been very much inflated in the west, so that one gets the idea here that the Buddha was just a practical man who refused to think. In fact, when he did talk philosophy he did it with such obvious delight and mastery that somebody, I think it was Trevor Ling, has called him "the most brilliant dialectician of his age". It was just these four stock questions that he refused to argue about, partly because the Brahmins spent their whole time doing so, rather like the mediaeval schoolmen.

C.B. I think he felt that our minds, in our present state of experience, were not ready to understand the answers even if they were given to them.

He wasn't interested in the question of creation. Yet I always think one of the most religious questions one can ask oneself is why there should be anything rather than nothing.

F.W. Yes, I agree. In early Buddhism this question is a meditation. As I said, the ancient myth of a creator god who formed a stretch of earth here, and a tree there, and water somewhere else is dismissed with a smile. The way it's understood in Buddhism is that we perceive things as trees and grass and so on because this is how our senses interpret them. Beings with a different sensing apparatus perceive material objects differently. And something else comes into it — it's usually called "grasping" (*tanha* is the Pali word for it: it's the second Noble Truth). It also has to do with affinity: we grasp at what we are capable of desiring. We, human beings, are said to perceive matter as we do because of a certain grossness in our present state of development. Beings with purer and more intense senses than ours interpret what is "out there" somewhat differently. They "grasp" too, but their experience is very different. Various metaphors which describe it express it as a spiritual delight far beyond anything we can normally conceive of. This is what the "heaven worlds" are, and there are higher worlds than those. But all these spheres — and it makes no difference whether they are very luminous or very gross and heavy (a lot of them are much sadder and darker than ours) — they all form part of what Buddhists call the "worlds" in which beings evolve and move about. Outside the whole of this system is the transcendence, which is the goal of the Path, and that is experienced when all forms of grasping cease, and only love and wisdom arise in the mind.

I thought you said that the Buddha discouraged metaphysical speculation.

F.W. Yes. The nature of the elements, or what is "out there", is a meditation. It's a seeing and intuiting, and nothing to do with thinking. It is not a meditation that I can do, incidentally. It calls for a very acute degree of spiritual penetration. And a Buddhist doesn't have to believe any of this unless, or until, he experiences it.

To what extent have Buddhists been concerned to update their thinking in the light of modern science? Modern Christianity has been very much concerned to try to understand its doctrines in the light, for example, of the theory of evolution. Has modern science ruffled the surface at all in Buddhism?

F.W. It is always said that it hasn't. For instance, the Indian mind has always conceived of aeon upon aeon of time, during which things have evolved. They also have this idea that things grow, and then decline and disappear, and then evolve and grow again. These ideas don't seem to clash with modern science.

C.B. I can't think of anything that Buddhism is trying to do that would be affected by the progress of modern science.

The impression I have got of the Buddha's own ideas about the nature and structure of the universe is that he anticipated many of the findings of modern physicists. He felt a sort of identification between matter and energy.

F.W. Yes. If one asks a learned Thera about the nature of objects the reply one usually gets is that although one can't understand them in the light of "Reality" they have some sort of phenomenal existence as centres of force.

And what about the psychological sciences?

F.W. Charles Tart in his book *Altered States of Consciousness* has some interesting points to make. Do you remember that nice story in his book about the blue vase? It was in some American university: an experimenter got some of his friends to do this piece of research for him. He had an empty room with just a carpet and a cushion, and a blue vase at the end of it. He asked his friends to go in, one by one, in the morning and in the evening, for ten minutes, and meditate on the vase. As they came out he took down what they said. The first time they went in they got it all wrong. One chap said, "I followed the contours of the vase", and another, "I imagined it with almond blossom in: I thought of it as a container." So he said: "Don't do that sort of thing; there's far too much cerebration or aesthetic feeling going on; just meditate as it were on the 'vasishness' of the vase". After these very vague instructions they went in next day and started again. Then some of them said, "I felt as if the vase and I were one", "I seemed to merge into the vase"; there was beautiful, pure Upanishadic stuff coming out. At the end of the week he took away the vase. They went into the room, and they all came out one after the other saying, "Where is the vase?" And he said, "Surely you don't need the vase now?" But they were all deeply upset about this: the vase had become a numinous object, you see. And this is quite in keeping with Buddhist ideas. You project the sense of the numinous and it plays back to you. It's this kind of experimentation that helps the meditator to know what he's up to, to know how he gets carried away by a sacred object.

Would this vase be a sort of raft?

F.W. Yes, but the fact that it becomes numinous for us is very important. This is perhaps why sacred places have this numinous quality; it's something that the mind has projected into them; yet it is a valid, objective quality as well.

When you say that the vase became for these people a numinous object, you mean, do you, that it became a vehicle of the numinous, that it meditated the numinous for them?

F.W. I suppose that might be said, yes.

Well now, the man who was conducting the experiment said they shouldn't have needed the vase any longer.

F.W. But he was only a man doing an experiment; he wasn't setting himself up as a guru. He wanted to find out what would happen, that's all.

My point is that I think the numinous is *mediated . . .*

F.W. You're talking about *the* numinous. Do you mean "God" by that?

I would want it to cover as broad a range of experience as possible. There is this experience which people call "the numinous". It may come through some particular thing; it may perhaps come through nothing. But I am rather sceptical about it's coming through nothing. And that's why I tend to feel that they did need the vase.

F.W. In the end I suppose you internalize the whole experience. From what I understand of Christian mysticism the mystics say (and this is why they are sometimes regarded as heretical) that they go beyond the personal, beyond the personal mediating figure of Christ, to what Buddhists would call the emptiness, and what Eckhardt I think called the "nothing" — though he didn't mean that in a negative sense; I think he meant the non-personal. It seems to be a quality of the mind that it can go beyond the mediating point, and this is the breakthrough into the absolute. I don't think it's necessary for everyone to follow this mystical line; it just suits some people. For others, a mediating person may be necessary. But in mysticism the mediating figure is passed beyond.

There is a sense, though, isn't there, in which we can't do without material things. Your whole self is constituted by your relationship to the world that you're in. I should have thought that, whatever direct mystical awareness a person may have, it's all conditioned beforehand by his experience of material things and of people. You can't start off in a vacuum, finding God as a purely interior experience. You wouldn't be a person if you didn't have all this previous experience, would you?

F.W. Yes; to start off you must have some kind of framework or ritual; and if one over-intellectualizes and throws away that framework it is a mistake. This is the point of believing in a religion: it gives you a framework of belief. This is why it is such a mistake to divorce meditation or any other of these techniques from any great tradition, and people who do it come a cropper.

Suppose this happens spontaneously, as in the case of a child where there hasn't been a chance for the establishment of any such framework, intellectual or emotional; yet there is still this sense of something greater which can come through a mere relationship with the world around us. Wordsworth felt this.

F.W. And then Wordsworth lost it.

Otto, who coined this word numinous, regarded it as referring to something objective; something outside the self. He said it should never be used as an adjective; one should not talk of things as numinous. He certainly does associate it with nature mysticism. (Writing ten years before Otto, Marrett the anthropologist outlined exactly what Otto called the numinous.) Otto uses the word to describe something in the universe that's really there, something one may make contact with in sacred buildings and in surroundings of great natural beauty. I myself have had such moments. I always remember the sunlight coming through young lime tree leaves; I remember the extraordinary sensation that came over me as a boy. And I still get this feeling from time to time. I don't think one need lose it really. Though Wordsworth did, as he became more and more of a conventional Christian. It's terrible to see the alterations he made in the 1850 edition of The Prelude *all to bring it into line with established theological doctrines.*

F.W. Perhaps he felt them to be true.

I always feel the earlier version reflects the numinous more vividly; it's a far more spiritual vision than the later one.

C.B. You mean then he was speaking from actual experiences, whereas later he was saying what he felt he ought to say.

Very much depends on how determined you are to keep that experience, that sense, and not to let it go, to live by it and perhaps grow with it.

Is there in fact in Buddhism any tradition of what we call "nature mysticism"?

F.W. I would say that in those early times people were so imbued with the beauty of nature that they hardly commented on it. They expressed it by saying, "The Devas walk the earth, and we talk with them." That was their relationship with the numinous if you like. Where I disagree with you is in this. Any sensitive person going for a country walk has these impressions, which one might call pantheistic, but I think they're childish. Unless you're a great religious genius, in order to deepen and solidify these feelings, to become adult and mature, I think you need the framework of a religious tradition.

I'm not really disagreeing with you at all, because when I was referring to the numinous I wasn't speaking only of "nature mysticism". You may have your first experience of the numinous in the context of nature, and as you grow it may be extended to other spheres of experience. Some people find it difficult to fit their personal experience into any accepted framework of tradition, or to commit themselves to any one particular raft.

May we turn to another question? Tibetan Buddhist monks seem to lay great emphasis on the need to have some kind of skill or craft: some are painters, some weavers, some musicians and so on. Is this emphasized in Zen or Theravada Buddhism?

C.B. Do you mean that the acquisition of this skill is to be regarded as part of the process of development?

I thought it was to be regarded rather as offering an alternative to a sole preoccupation with meditation.

C.B. Well Buddhist monks don't sit all day in meditation. They have to cook and clean and do all the gardening, and go out begging.

Well is there any importance given to the development of any craft or profession?

C.B. Not necessarily, though if anyone turns up at a Zen monastery who is a very good cook for instance his abilities will be welcome. If somebody comes who is a very good calligrapher there will be time for him to practise. But I've never heard of anyone learning to become a stonemason, or actually cultivating any such craft inside a monastery. Though of course a lay person would be perfectly capable of doing that, and making such a development part of his religious life. The whole of his life could be concentrated in the cultivation of one particular form of perfection, woodcarving or calligraphy, or whatever you like.

Is there an emphasis on finding a rhythm? You know the Benedictine tradition: so many hours of this and so many hours of that, so that the mind learns a rhythm that helps the life of meditation.

C.B. I've never heard it actually stated, but of course they don't sit all day in meditation. The only times when they do sit at it for long hours are the retreats called Sesshin. Then the whole point is to build up energy. But quite frankly, and I think Freda may agree with me, there are only two people that I know who have become better, nicer, more balanced, less unpleasant than they were before as a result of doing Zen. I'm speaking of Westerners now of course. All the others I have known of have become definitely worse. It's interesting that I was told that nowadays the Zen disciple is given far more definite instruction. Compare Dr. Suzuki's training. Once about nine years ago I went to see Dr. Suzuki. Christmas Humphreys had said, "If you possibly can, get him to write his memoirs. We'd love to know about his early experiences, and how he came into Zen." So I went to see the old man, who was then about 90, and asked, could he not try to write his autobiography. "Well", he said, "I'm too tired and too old, and I've got too much to do." Then I said, "I suppose you couldn't dictate it, could you?" And he said, "All right; let's start now." So the splendid Japanese girl who was acting as his secretary and nurse and companion and cook went off and got pen and paper, and he started at once. He went on dictating for about an hour; then he got tired. I went away, read it through and typed it out, and the next day came back and read it out to him. As a result, in a week, we got a most interesting description of somebody who had done their Zen training in the early 1890's. He described how he was given the Koan, often assigned to beginners, the one called "Joshu's Mu". A monk once asked Joshu whether a dog also had the Buddha nature, and Joshu answered "Mu". Usually Mu means "no". But you're told it doesn't mean "no"; it has no meaning at all. Then why did Joshu say it? We were told not to give it any figurative or metaphorical meaning but just to concentrate on "Mu, Mu, Mu, Mu, Mu." But Dr. Suzuki was given no help whatsoever. He used to go into the Master's room and attempt to give an answer; the Master would then ring a little bell and say, "Out!" This went on for a whole year. The Master would never say anything to him, not a single word. But instead of being discouraged — after all, most people would just fall by the wayside — with Dr. Suzuki, the method worked, because it roused in him a terrific spiritual endeavour. He remembers sitting in his garden and thinking, "If I can't find out what "Mu" means, I'd rather die". And this energy grew and grew. He would go to the retreats every month, and twice a day he would go to the Master for instruction. Every time it was just "Out!" Then suddenly, he said, in the very cold December retreat, the truth suddenly burst upon him and he rushed to the Master. The Master, you may remember, at this juncture asks certain questions that you have to answer: "Show me Mu on a mountain", "Cut Mu in half", "Show me Mu in the middle of the road", and that kind of thing. Each Master has his own questions. For Dr. Suzuki, this was a true experience. The method worked with him. But let's face it, it wouldn't work for most people. It's just that he was ideally fitted for it. His energy was roused by the total impasse.

And at the time was this method supposed to work with everybody?

C.B. Yes, at that time.

It wasn't meant as a method of selection?

C.B. Well I suppose those people it didn't work with just left. There was a famous Japanese novelist called Natsume Soseki who in one of his novels described how he went to that very temple and was given that Koan, and how he was completely baffled by it. This was about 1890. This was the traditional Rinzai way: they gave no help whatsoever. But I still feel that it's not for many western people; at least only for a very small minority.

9

Raynor Johnson

The title of your book The Imprisoned Splendour* *comes from a poem Browning wrote when he was a young man* — Paracelsus. *Perhaps I could read the passage:*

Truth is within ourselves; it takes no rise
From outward things, whate'er you may believe.
There is an inmost centre in us all,
Where truth abides in fulness; and around,
Wall upon wall, the gross flesh hems it in,
This perfect, clear perception — which is truth.
A baffling and perverting carnal mesh
Binds it and makes all error: and to KNOW
Rather consists in opening out a way
Whence the imprisoned splendour may escape,
Than in effecting entry for a light
Supposed to be without.

Now if you compare that with what he wrote thirty years later, in Rabbi Ben Ezra, *you find he'd changed his mind somewhat. For instance, he was no longer so ready to accept the body as a "perverting carnal mesh"; now he could write:*

Let us not always say
"Spite of this flesh to-day
I strove, made head, gained ground upon the whole".
As the bird wings and sings
Let us cry "All good things
Are ours, nor soul helps flesh more now than flesh helps soul."

Would you say that you too had had any kind of second thoughts, or had changed your views in any such way?

**Hodder, 1953*

Raynor Johnson

I don't think if I had to rewrite the book now that I'd change it very much. It's difficult to say. Shall I tell you something of my own sort of pilgrimage?

Yes, please do.

I read Physics at Oxford. I don't know why. I came up in 1919 and found myself a very callow, raw, homesick, youth, with a number of officers just returned from the first World War. I felt very shy; I wasn't mature enough to benefit from Oxford as I should have done. I wasted, well, I lost a lot of time. Then I got attracted by spectroscopy. When I went out to Melbourne I found that it would be very difficult to get time free from my administration to get the prolonged periods to research, so I dropped research, and said good-bye to my special field. Then I met one or two rather extraordinary people, one of whom I've written about, a friend, Ambrose Pratt. He was an Australian and had some unusual psychical gifts. For example, he'd always seen auras, clearly, round the human body, from childhood upwards, and could moreover interpret them; he knew what these things meant. He had also acquired, as a young man, the power of astral projection, about which I knew nothing at the time. He used to use this, especially during the war period, when he'd go out of his body, find out what he wanted, and come back. He was a very fascinating person. He had a great appreciation of Eastern thought and Eastern religions, and this fired by own interest. Furthermore, I saw that he had these unusual powers of a psychical kind, which he sometimes talked to me about, and I thought, "Well, it's up to me now to get out of this materialistic bias and pursue further psychical research." I didn't do much of a practical, experimental kind, but I did cover the literature through the Journal and the Proceedings of the Society for Psychical Research. The bulk of it was enormous, but I went through it to know what it was all about, and in the process of doing this I found myself. I saw the mystic side, got some sense of the mystic at work, and of mystical experience, and how it related to those who had some kind of psychic knowledge, and this appealed to me inwardly. I said to myself, "This is what I'm hungry for, I want it"; so that if I had to be labelled, which I wouldn't like to be, I feel I would call myself a mystic. The main disciplines of life have been taking up a good bit of time. You can call them yoga or what you like. You have to live a disciplined life; you have to balance the meditation, the inward search, with whatever unselfish help you can give to those around, and this is the chief thing I have attempted.

Raynor Johnson

About 12 years ago there came to my front door a person whom I hadn't met before, and who just said, "You don't know me, Dr. Johnson, but I know you". I said, "Well, will you come in", and we sat and talked in my study for quite a time. I realised immediately that I was in the presence of a very unusual and remarkable person, for whom I couldn't help but feel intuitively great respect. This person I have been in touch with since, and I now realise (what I took some little time to realise) that this person was a very great teacher. So I've been under direction of what you would call a guru, or a Messenger, or a Master. I've had the great advantage of direction in the matter of things of the spirit. The situation frankly is that in the West these great beings who've got no obligation to be here on the planet at all, except their own wish to do the Father's work, these great beings work quietly. All this talk about gurus and what-not, and collecting a month's salary, and that kind of thing young people are so keen on today, is nonsense; because no true Master would ever claim to be such, nor would he allow his followers to say that. They're working in the Western world as secretly and quietly as they can. The situation in India and certain Eastern countries is quite different — a holy man is revered and respected and not harassed, not criticised. There's a recognition and devotion to his quality at large, so that a man may operate there in some degree more openly. In the West it's different; he'd be far more likely to be shot as a dangerous person.

Don't you think the atmosphere in the West is changing?

I really doubt that. It seems a shocking thing to say, but I'm sure if a Great One came, and it was known who he was, the Church would be one of his strongest opponents. It would be the old, old story of 2,000 years ago. The hierarchy who want to keep their power would be very suspicious of anyone who could speak from first-hand experience, and all down the ages the Church has been strongly suspicious of its mystics, because they were speaking from first-hand experience, and this was a challenge to traditional orthodoxy. Do you know that passage in *Pilgrim's Progress* where the Pilgrim is setting off on his journey, and he asks a character called Evangelist the correct way to go. He asks him, "Can you see the wicket gate over yonder?" "No", he says; "Well, can you see that light?" and he replies, "I think I do. "Well", says Evangelist, "go over to the light and then you'll see the gate." Now, I feel that intellect has limitations. I've become increasingly strongly aware of this. It may be because I'm getting older (I'm 74), but I do feel that intellect has done its real work for us when it's pointed out the wicket gate and said, "You can safely go through that gate, and you won't regret it." That's been the experience I've had. I feel that after you've done that, it's much more a search at a deep level within. It goes beyond intellect. And the actual process of using one's mind to the best of one's ability, well, I think it's important to do that first, almost, if I may put it crudely, to get it out of the system. Can I put it this way: I think you have to walk as a mystic under the archway of humility all the time, or you can't hope to approach the Presence; and also that you have in your hands the two keys of love and trust, and these will open all doors for you. That's what my Teacher once said to me, and I feel it was a bit of great wisdom.

Yes, I would agree. There are all sorts of things science cannot touch; but I do maintain that we can use the scientific method to study the written records, and so make the intellectual world realise, by the methods of science, that religion is something of vital importance to man.

Would you think it wise to make a distinction here between religion, religious experience, and spirituality?

Well, I'd say that the essence of religious experience is a kind of spiritual awareness. What I call religious experience is being in contact with something that appears to be beyond the surface, something transcendental.

Yes. I feel, for example, that when Paul said "I live, yet not I, but Christ within me", the "I" that he repeats is different. "I live", but not the ego part of me, but the higher self he referred to as "Christ liveth in me", and I feel he was just saying the same thing as the Eastern philosophers are saying when they talk about the Atman.

The same as Browning was saying when he says "Truth is within ourselves"? I'd rather like to take you up on this, because our correspondents did, after all, answer an appeal to "all those who felt that their lives had been affected by some power beyond *themselves"; and a large number of them have insisted that basically truth is* not *within outselves, it comes from outside, or from beyond, or something like this. They don't have this feeling that truth is within ourselves and that all they have to do is to find it; but they feel they must lay themselves open to it; it must come from outside.*

I think there's a problem of semantics here. If you look with the eyes of the senses, and the part of the mind that interprets the data of the senses, it may give one reply; but the waters of a spring, which is bubbling up in the earth which they can see, are from a hidden part. In other words, surely at the deepest point of ourselves, what ever you want to call it, the Self with a capital S or the soul, the light is within *that*; and it isn't our own light, it's a light from beyond. To use theological language, "the Light that lighteth every man that cometh into the world" is not one's own private possession, it's a loan to one as it were; it's a part of the unity of the great light. When I think about the soul, I'm a bit Jungian in my thinking. Jung talks about the deep centre, doesn't he? He doesn't talk about the soul. If the soul is a lamp, our chief business is to keep the lamp trimmed, but the light within the lamp isn't ours; it's a part of the great light, the Holy Spirit. I don't know whether I've quite met your point, have I?

Yes, well, it's all very paradoxical; as you say, language fails.

Yes, because what is objective on one level is subjective on another.

I think there's a sort of dialectic. If one thinks continually in terms of inwardness, and the individual soul and so on, one has a sense of sustaining integrity and so on; and yet I feel we're not really like that. We live in a sort of co-inherence with other people, with other men, and a part of the truth is revealed between *man and man, and not just to single persons. It's a dialectical event.*

I increasingly feel, as I look at the different religions of the world, that the chief differences between them are where they draw the line and say, "That's immanence" and "That's transcendence". You know, the point at which they make their emphasis. When the Buddha said "Be ye lamps unto yourselves", he was drifting strongly towards immanence, and so the Eastern religions do; but orthodox Christianity tends to feel that God is out there, and high up, to be worshipped. I feel that to have the truth, the two parts have got to be put together.

There have been many attempts to express this within Christianity. A good deal of traditional Trinitarian theology we have to see as an attempt to deal with this concept that we're all basically one.

Yes. It is the unity of the core of all religions that impresses one increasingly, and not the differences. I have a strong feeling that it's one great Soul who appears at one time as Jesus and at another time as Gautama (and I could go on and on) in a manifestation appropriate to the time and the place, but that's pure speculation. One of the difficulties in discussing mystical experience is that of formulating it in words. One tends when one looks at these accounts to recognise that one person may have a very considerable facility of expression, and it doesn't follow that, because one is so persuaded and so moved by the quality of the writing, that it's a deeper expression of it. That is one difficulty, in putting it into words which are the symbols; and then the second difficulty, I feel, is this: sometimes people write to one, and say, "I have had this experience", and I'm always a little bit uncomfortable, in a curious way; a very interested recipient, but an uncomfortable recipient, because I have an inner feeling that the deeper forms of mystical experience — you might not agree with me — one shouldn't attampt to exteriorise, and that if one does, one is liable to cut oneself off, or to make it more difficult for the Spirit, or whatever you want to call It, to indwell again. I think one is doing some kind of — violence is too strong a word, but one is doing some kind of injustice to talk about the very sacred. You are exposing something of the highest quality to — I'm putting it crudely — to the criticism, the interpretation of the intellectuals, etc. I think this is another difficulty.

Yes, it is a difficulty, I think, but many of those who write to us say straight out, "An experience like that I cannot describe, but it had the most tremendous effect on me." There is the evidence that interests us. We don't expect a person to put onto paper in words something that is quite ineffable, but we want to collect the evidence, to show that there is a power which people can get by some particular kind of prayer or approach, to show that here is something really important in man's development; people's lives can be changed, they can get the strength and power to do things they would not otherwise be able to do.

Have you any views as to why Jung is not more studied in the Universities? Why is Freud academically respectable, and Jung neglected so much?

Because, I think, psychology has tended towards a behaviourist type of approach, people tend to think of Freud's method as more scientific. But again I think there's change coming there. Although I must say I find myself in great sympathy with Jung, I find it extremely difficult to understand what he's saying a great deal of the time. The idea of the collective unconscious — I can never get a Jungian to tell me exactly what is meant by it. You'd think at times he was thinking as if the collective unconscious of all of us was connected in this way, horizontally; at other times you'd think the shared unconscious was going back genetically, racially, right back to the ancestral archetypes. Well now, these are two entirely different concepts. Sometimes he talks as if he's talking of one, and sometimes the other. Which does he really mean?

I don't think they're incompatible with each other. I see your distinction, but aren't they as necessary to each other as any two of the dimensions in a three or four-dimensional world? His archetypal world is part of all the know-how of nature, as well as an accumulation of experience. It goes deep, but like a carrot, it spreads out as it grows up.

There's another aspect of Jung's thought that I find difficult. It seems to me that when he talks about individuation, this is a kind of religious process, that people can find themselves, and integrate themselves, and that this is a religious search. Now part of that individuation, if I understand it, is to absorb the shadow, as Jung calls it, into yourself, to be aware of it, and this is the dark side, this is evil. I find it very difficult to reconcile this process with a mystical, religious point of view. Do you see what I mean? Because it's an individual, almost a selfish process, to try to realise yourself. Perhaps it's a way of understanding and growing, yet in a way it seems it's putting a great stress on yourself and your own personal qualities. There's also this problem of the shadow, which I find very hard to understand from a religious point of view.

You remember the old advice, "Know thyself". The first level one gets into is the nearer level of the unconscious. There one sees how much one has tucked away through one's life, how the stuff we didn't want to face in ourselves is there; and so much of this is shadow stuff. I think one has to know what one is; and to *know* includes not only the conscious knowledge but the unconscious too. Jung makes the point, as you remember, that in gaining this knowledge, and in reacting rightly to how we really are, we find the shadow turns from black to grey, and maybe perhaps some day to white. This self-knowledge, I think, is important. I feel that the process of individuation that Jung stresses is very close to the mystic's path. The chief difference, it seems to me, is that he doesn't stress love in the way that Christian religion does, and which the Buddha does by his compassion. Jung tends, as a psychiatrist, to hesitate to speak as forcibly as he should on that subject. But he makes amends for it in one chapter of *Memories, Dreams, Reflections*, as you know, where you can see he's almost worshipping but he doesn't talk about it because he can't find words.

You spoke of mystical experience, and describe yourself as a mystic. Would you say that the capacity for mystical experience is one which is universal to humanity, or would you say it was confined only to a few?

Well, the potentiality is there in all, but its development and evolution to a point where it's recognised is confined to only a few, but it's there, all the time, in all; just as every acorn, I'm sure, has the potential in it of becoming an oak-tree, given the right environment in which it's planted.

Well, what do you think we should do about our environment?

Well, what *can* one do? Except fertilise it, by which I mean show as much loving and caring and helpfulness as one can to one's fellows, on the assumption that basically we're all one, we're all linked. On the outer level in the senses we're separate in characteristics, but the deeper you go into reality, the more you're aware of unity. You become aware of it with psychical phenomena; that's a relatively superficial depth, but the deeper you go into it, the more you are aware of the great unity of all.

It seems to me that our educational system doesn't always encourage this attitude. It does seem that much of our educational tradition is concerned with intellectual analysis and with knowledge rather than with the understanding of that part of oneself by which one becomes aware of the great unity.

I accept that fully.

But if the Church exists to help people to become more religious, perhaps it is the function of the Church rather to develop this aspect of man's nature, and help it to grow.

I'm just a little unhappy about the sentence "the Church exists to help man to become more religious", unless we mean by "becoming more religious" that contact with higher levels of consciousness which ultimately will lead to full awareness of God.

Well, this seems to me a very good definition of what religion's all about, but other people might not accept it.

Yes.

There was a question earlier about the distinction between the religious and the spiritual. How would you answer that question yourself?

I've always felt that all the great mystics were men who had had first hand, immediate contact with Reality, or God, whatever that means, and that very few of their followers could come up to that level, though here and there a man reaches the same inner knowledge, by which I mean definite knowledge, not speculative knowledge. This is a little inner core, and it's the central element, the essence of all religions; but relatively few of their followers have that first-hand knowledge. Then as time passes you get all the philosophers, the priests, the theologians very busy discussing what the founder really meant — you know, the analytical approach; hence your theology. And I suppose St. Paul was the first of the theologians, in the Christian tradition. At any rate he had most to say. Just in parenthesis, I've always been staggered to reflect that as far as I can see, St. Paul had never heard the teachings of Jesus; he mentions none of the parables, he doesn't mention many of the things that most concern us today; he was a typical theologian; he started to speculate, philosophise, and build up his own ideas about what he understood Jesus stood for, but if he'd ever heard of the parable of the Prodigal Son there's no indication of it in his writings. However, that's by the way. I think you've got this intellectual level of religion, in which theologians conflict with each other, and have their happy times; you've got the level where, I think, the emotions are involved, the devotional level, where one finds many good people, who haven't perhaps at present the *capacity* for mystical experience, and are certainly not intellectuals; yet they can participate in the fellowship of the religious. Then on the outer level we've got all the rituals, the organisations, and so on. So when one talks of religion, I think of these four different levels. When I was talking in India at the end of '62 for a short time, the first thing that was said to me by one of the persons who was with me, was, "May I suggest that you carefully differentiate between religion and spirituality?" The theme I was supposed to be talking on was "Science and Spirituality". I must have dropped into the use of "Science and Religion". He was more or less politely telling me, "Be very careful which term you use, because here religion can include a lot of things not necessary to spirituality." I took his point; I thought it was a good one.

When you talk about those levels, do you feel they're getting progressively further away from the real thing?

Oh, indeed I do.

I mean, the devotional level, for instance; I'm not sure if I've quite understood what you mean by it.

I think it's what would be represented by Bhakti Yoga in India. There are a lot of people who participate in religious observances on the level of their emotions. They say, "I *feel* close to God, I feel this, or I feel the other", and to them this devotional attitude towards the things that they hear and the atmosphere in which they worship is of more importance. Many of these are simple folk, but one honours them.

But aren't they sometimes closer to the real thing than those who live on the doctrinal level?

Well, without casting aspersions on the theologians, I would say yes, often a great deal nearer.

For many people, again, what appears to be the rather formal and artificial ceremonial is a necessary means of getting to the higher level.

I recognise that, so I feel that one shouldn't be critical in any way or despise any other tradition at all. To aspire to the heights one has to make use of every aid and help that one can, and what might not appeal to oneself may be a great aid and help to others. My own affinity on the religious level would be with the Quakers rather than, shall I say, the Greek Orthodox or the Roman Catholic, but that's just a temperamental peculiarity of mine, probably based upon experiences in a past life.

You said that the basic difference between the different religions is shown by the line which is drawn between immanence and transcendence; but how does this work out in reality? If you look at the different religions, and the different societies in which they flourish, you can see that there is much more than simply a difference of emphasis on either transcendence or immanence. You think that we ought to have a sort of individualistic approach, and that mystical experience is based on the individual experience, isn't that so?

The mystical approach *is*, you might say, basically individual. But this is paradoxical: the farther you go, as an individual, the less you *are* an individual, in other words you realise increasingly the sense of unity with all. It's a paradoxical thing, the more you withdraw from the environment, in the sense of going deeper within, or higher, lifting your consciousness, the more you are aware of your unity with the all. The poets express this far better than I can do, so I won't press the point. Immanence and transcendence, one's got to hold both of these two together. The theologians know it. The emphasis of the Buddha, for example, was very practical. I know if you look at the scriptures that have been left behind by his enthusiastic followers he seems to become highly metaphysical, but I think, just as Jesus was, he was concerned with very practical things. He never really philosophised, or went into the question of life after death, or the different levels of the consciousness; he was concerned with being helpful to ordinary people, to help them build up an idea out of their limited thoughts, to show them how one should be able to live. Buddha wasn't known as the All-Compassionate One for nothing.

Do you think, when you're making this point about transcendence and immanence, that in fact it really matters? For example, if you stress the transcendence, you get this "wholly otherness", and if you stress the immanence, you get over on to the pantheistic side. I've always myself felt that if you get a balance you are really arriving at something that expresses to me the true form of the personal. This is why, as a Christian, I have a particular interest in the experience of this power, this spiritual power outside ourselves as a personal power, because in fact it is both beyond and it is within; and therefore I am always puzzled by the sort of Eastern tradition in which the personal doesn't seem to matter. I wonder what you think about this?

I think you've got to hold both sides. I think the great ones are enlightened, in that they have had, on a high or a deep level, an immediate conscious awareness of God. He is a reality to them, so that although, being incarnate, they can't live on that high level, they can at any time withdraw, as it were, from their senses, from the surrounding world, and rise through the levels of consciousness and become fully, consciously aware of their unity with the Divine. But I think the immanence and transcendence have both got to be held. I feel the stress of the Buddha was laid rather on immanence. When he said, "Be ye lamps unto yourselves", for example, he was recognising the soul, or the self, if you like, as a lamp within which the divine light would shine, and he was virtually saying, "If you take that light as your guide in all the relationships of life, you won't go wrong". I think Jesus was putting the emphasis a little more in the middle, and the orthodox developments have tended towards transcendence. As you know, He is the worshipped, I am only a creature; He is the creator, and as a result we get prayer as the characteristic intimate activity of the Christian, while as a result of the Buddhist emphasis, meditation is the characteristic inner activity of the Buddhist, because the Buddha says, God is deep within me, and by withdrawing as far as I can, I shall get near to that point which is God. But both are true; it's paradoxical, but the ways are linked, it's the same goal in the end. But please, I'm only just thinking aloud; I don't hold any of these views dogmatically, I do want to say that. One feels one is completely mixed up; one feels these things are live, and you can only be terribly humble when you talk about them.

10

Michael Whiteman

Perhaps I could start by putting to you a question that frequently arises in our work. Again and again people write to us describing experiences which they say are ineffable, which cannot be described — and yet they feel an irresistible compulsion to try to describe them. Now you speak in your book of a "level of self-evident reality". If this is as objectively and commonly attainable as you imply, how is it that people find it so difficult to describe?*

In such cases the things that people are trying to describe are difficult to communicate merely because they are very unfamiliar; the words of ordinary language don't seem at first to fit; one has to grow into new uses of them. After all, it's not a thing that you can just open the door to and then you've got it. The whole progress towards spiritual things is very elaborate and complicated: it demands a remaking of oneself, and one has to forge a language, so to speak, on the way, in order to find the words to express things that are at first so unfamiliar. I've always differed rather strongly from people who lay such emphasis on the ineffability of mystical experience. William James, for instance, to my mind laid too much emphasis on this. I think an experience at a high level, shall we say, is said to be ineffable by people who are so struck by the differences from ordinary experience that at first all they can think of is: "I must stress this difference; it's so totally different from ordinary physical or psychological experience that words fail me." But they would never have recognised the experience as being different from the physical unless something had got through that was *recognizably* different, whether it's a sort of universality or whether it's the transformation of themselves. Something has come through, but they can't at that moment catch hold of suitable words. I would say that always if one has any high-level experience one has a distinct tendency to put it into words somehow, because one has to give it

**The Mystical Life* (Faber, 1961)

ground in oneself. If you didn't give it ground in yourself you'd lose it; you'd forget it. We can't get away from this tendency. It's necessary for our own development and also because the experience is too valuable a thing to lose straight away. So I'd rather say that the tendency to call a thing ineffable is the result of the initial shock of coming up against something one can't quite catch hold of in words. One hasn't developed sufficiently; one hasn't formed a language which will fit. But it will come; it *must* come, because any experience that really belongs to us, that we can really understand, that means something to us, *must* have this ground in language. So I would take with several grains of salt any statement of a mystic that his experience was too great in certain respects for him quickly to find language which was at all up to the greatness of the experience; every word in every language is, I would say, inadequate. But you put up with an inadequate word. You make a sort of allowance; you say, "Well, for my purposes this word is sufficient, but if you're going to argue about it of course it's going to be inadequate."

You mean that this is true even in the scientific sphere? That we make models out of words which are inadequate, but they do for us?

Yes, that's right. If we talk about particles in physics, we have to make a whole world of reservations: we don't really mean a particle in the usual sense. In the same way in mysticism, if we talk of God as being transcendent we have to make reservations. But within ourselves we know what we mean by it.

Can I go back behind this to ask what you think about the way things are perceived? Are you saying, as I understand John Oman to say, that we perceive the supernatural as well as the natural directly, intuitively in some sense? That they are both givennesses of our experience, for everybody?

Yes, there must be a givenness in mystical experience. Otherwise it ceases to have what I would call mystical quality.

But in that case why is the experience of the supernatural so much out of the range of most people's experience? You seem to be saying that the way to it is a complex one, the way to the mystical experience, but that disordered flashes may come to anybody. Is that so?

Yes, I think that's a good way of putting it.

Would you say there is some sort of faculty in man for perceiving it, similar to our faculty for perceiving the physical world, which is ill-developed, or which has become atrophied in some way?

It's not exactly a faculty — well, perhaps with some reservations one could call it a faculty; I was going to say something more like a *technique*. What I'm trying to get away from is the psychological view that we have a sort of "feeling" for this. It's something that has to be developed in us. It's developed by a kind of self-control. But the way is extremely complicated. We may be progressing along an orderly line without realising it. And people's lines of progress may be so different that what may seem orderly to one person may seem quite disorderly to another because he can't see where the different steps are leading. And so what may seem to one person a flash that comes out of the blue may actually be some peculiar step that is needed for him. It had a past, and it will have an effect in the future. Another person who perhaps has the same sort of experience in a more controlled way must not be thought of as having necessarily progressed further along the way. It's only that it is the result of his way of life or his background that he should have developed certain techniques which lead to the revelation being more continuous, more under control. Whereas the other person who gets the flash is working so to speak in the dark because it's for his good; it's his way of life to work in the dark and receive the light in flashes. It needs a very special background, a special attitude to life, a special purpose in life, to develop the necessary powers, the necessary techniques and outlook which will result in these things being more continuous. One can't take a person at random and say, "You should work in this way, and then you'll get these revelations continuously". It may be quite foreign to his needs. One mustn't make comparisons between people; I feel that very strongly. One person may get a continuous type of mystical revelation; another may get flashes. In either case the working has to go on, so to speak, behind the scenes, in a way that's very difficult to discern.

Are there any guide-lines that can be laid down, for one person by another?

I think it's very difficult to say what any one person should do, unless you have some indication that he has already progressed on the way to a certain point. Then you can perhaps make some suggestions: "Now I think this might be a good way to proceed", or "This, I think, is where you've gone wrong; you might try it out this way". One of the chief guide-lines is that one must view spiritual progress as first of all a matter of self-discipline. Every step in the way is some kind of self-discipline. It's not only a self-discipline as regards emotions; it must be a self-discipline as regards thought, belief, sense, everything, because as long as we have a lack of self-discipline, a lack of clarity, then we are entangled, we are tied up in ourselves, we lack spiritual freedom, and the most we can expect is some kind of flash which we should very quickly lose or distort because we had no control.

This is the state you call fixation?

Yes, we are all a mass of fixations, and essentially the mystical way is to release these fixations one by one until there comes a time when they are released without effort, because our response has become open and unified.

Does this come about because we ourselves are inclined to this or that aspect of reality? Our own inclinations must play some part at the start.

Yes; but I think it is important to stress that such inclinations are the opposite of wishful thinking. Wishful thinking is one of the fixations which the mystic must be particularly on guard against, which he must overcome. We have to watch inside ourselves unceasingly. If a thought comes, we must say, as it were: "Now this is a thought presenting itself", or "It's a belief". We must not say, "I think this", or "I believe this" (except perhaps as a mere form of words for purposes of communication). There is a world of difference between saying, "I feel this, I believe that, I think this", and saying, "The thought is before me; I will examine it, open myself to its intuitive character." It is in the difference between these attitudes that the essence of the mystical lies. You must have a *disinclination* to say, "This is mine". You must feel the *need* to release yourself, to stand apart, saying, as it were, "Something is presented; what is it?" Whether it's a thought, whether it's a feeling, whether it's a belief, all must be perceived in an open, released state. This is certainly not wishful thinking, not argumentation of any kind. Even if anything which I have said comes into your mind, and you think, "Ah, now, he said this", you should immediately take an objective viewpoint such as I have tried to describe. Say, rather, "This is a point of view", open your mind, and let intuition come in. What we have to get away from, for mystical perception, is the reasoning attitude of mind, the discursive attitude: one point, then another one, and then that one follows. Our state is not mystical until we have got beyond that discursive view of knowledge.

But isn't the discursive attitude necessary to co-ordinate the mystical with the rest of experience?

Yes, it's necessary as a foundation; it's necessary as a tool for progress; it's necessary for communication. But it's not the method of mystical insight.

Could you not be accused of putting the mystical into a separate department where it becomes untouchable by discursive criticism? The criticism for instance that all this just comes to you out of your own subconscious?

Naturally such an accusation will be levelled by all sorts of people; to them intuition is something subjectively "cooked up", while argument is "objective". But if one knows what the insight is that stands apart from objects of knowledge while contemplating them, one can find a ready answer to the accusation. A mystic will be struggling all the time — or shall we say, *searching* all the time — to see what is in the other person's attitude that leads him to such a wrong belief. If, for instance, somebody said, in reference to my mystical descriptions, "That's all very well, but you're just telling us your subjective psychological reactions", I might say, "On what ground do you say that these insights were 'subjective'?". I'm turning the point, you see; I'm trying to get inside his mind and expose his own fixations. I might go on to say, "It's you that are subject to prepossessions; you are grasping at a wrong view of the type of experience I am trying to describe. You have a theory built in at the back of your mind by trains of discursive reasoning. You are absorbed in the reactions, 'I feel this, I think that'. It's you that are subjective, you that are wrapped up in yourself. The mystic does away with that attitude. It is the mystic who impartially and penetratingly observes states of givenness and knowledge." In such a way one turns the tables. The charge of subjectivity is shown to arise from the critic's own fixated view, which blinds him to the possibility of objective insight. At the same time, we may freely admit that the mystic's verbal *descriptions* and *explanations* are open to discursive criticism, if this is well-founded.

Would you say then that the mystic is working within the framework of what Polanyi would call the framework of commitment? He avoids subjectivity by saying that in a situation of commitment you have got the personal pole, which is subjective (it's got to be true for you), and you have got the objective pole: there's something impersonally there which you wish to make contact with. Anyone who is what he calls an objectivist rejects this kind of talk about a commitment-framework. But would you agree that there are always these two poles, the objective and the subjective?

Partly. But this is one of those oppositions that virtually disappear in mysticism. Commitment and objectivity must in a sense both be present: one must be totally committed, and one must be totally detached. This means that whatever is whole-heartedly perceived by the subject has an objective character. If one can realise what it means to be totally committed and totally detached, one has come near to the mystical viewpoint.

This is surely a Buddhist view.

Buddhism is mysticism in its purest form; it is neat mysticism. Let me put it like this. If you say, "I am detached", it is almost certain that you are thinking fixatedly: "I am standing apart, I'm myself, and *that* which I am thinking about or observing is something else over against me." This is wrong. On the other hand, if you say, "I am totally committed", then the probability is that you are thinking: "I'm involved in it, I'm caught up in it." That is also a fixation. Neither manner of speech, separately, suggests quite the right viewpoint. This is a case where we must study the language we use and not take it too literally; this is where the "ineffability" comes in. A mystic will realise that is it misleading to call the right view either committed or detached. It's both, or neither. By saying "both committed and detached" I think we have a language tool to suggest an idea of the right attitude to other people, if we're lucky. Here again language appears as a tool for communication; it cannot be exact.

One finds the same kind of contradiction in personal relationships, doesn't one? A relationship of love between two people is one of both commitment and detachment.

Yes; anything that is of a higher value has to have those qualities. We have to be committed to a thing to the extent of really being inside it, of living it; but we have to be detached to the extent that we are not caught up in self and therefore clouded over and blinded.

Buber would say that such a view supports the idea that reality is essentially personal, and that our relationship to reality should be of the "I-Thou" kind. Would you agree?

I would agree in saying that all mysticism is knowledge of the personal; but of course some people would take the word "personal" to imply "wrapped up in oneself". I take it in a universal sense. Perhaps to say reality is not impersonal would be a better way of putting it.

I wonder whether you would say a little more about your mystical paradigm?

I would say that some germ of the experience which I take as a chief paradigm — the experience of God as transcendent — must be present and powerful in a person if he is to have any idea of what I call the mystical. Without some sense of God as transcendent I think it's going to sound rather strange to call an experience mystical or even religious. It's true God can be felt as immanent in us, but somehow however strong this sense of immanence is it doesn't seem quite so "religious", the word doesn't seem so appropriate, as when we think of God as transcendent. The knowledge of God as transcendent is in some ways the key knowledge of all.

And if we are to talk about people's needs being met, one must assume some kind of transcendence that answers to these needs.

Without the transcendence we are wrapped up in self; we are working things out under our own steam, by reasoning and so on. The transcendent has to be there as a superior wisdom, showing us the way, telling us what we must do. It's the transcendent to which we must be obedient, to which we are turned, which organises our life, which tells us what step is right next.

How can you be sure that this transcendent really is transcendent and not just part of your purely subjective thoughts?

We are in some ways like scientific experimenters: we are all eyes, all ears; and when a thing is presented to us in that state, the best answer I think is to say that there's no possible mistaking. If you really know God as transcendent, the idea of thinking of the experience as merely subjective is too laughable: it would never occur to you. But if it did, there would be a thousand reasons which would at once occur to show that the idea that it was just subjective was preposterous.

Why is there a necessary contradiction between subjective and objective?

The "purely" subjective (that is, fixatedly so) contradicts the detachedly objective. I am here accepting the term "subjective" more or less in its ordinary sense, as referring to something which is thought to be obviously in me and not in you, and implying "wrapped up in myself". It implies a kind of fixation. And so I'm saying that if one has a true perception of God as transcendent one automatically perceives that one is not fixated on self: transcendence and fixation are in complete and utter contradiction.

But can this transcendence ever be described in communicable terms?

One can always describe it in terms which are sufficiently satisfactory to oneself. Whether you can convey it in any way to another person depends on what his equipment is. If there's nothing in his experience to which you can appeal, then of course you can't make a mark. You have to search out the other person's background and find a word that calls forth some sort of response, whether "unity", or "exaltation", or "purity", or "transcendence". Some of these words must make a mark, otherwise you'll not communicate anything of it.

Then you would say that there's nobody who hasn't got some *sort of point from which one can start, to communicate this idea of transcendence?*

Yes, everyone must have some such point. It could be merely a matter of conscience, or of awareness of beauty; even of one's awareness of oneself, a kind of self-consciousness. All these things have deep within them some sort of awareness of the ultimate; they wouldn't seem real otherwise.

You seemed earlier on to use the word "psychological" with rather derogatory overtones. Could you say a little more about what you mean when you talk about things happening at a psychological level?

I use this word psychological for the bottom of my three levels: there's the psychological; then there's the intermediate or psychical level; and the highest is the strictly religious or mystical level. The lowest level is the level of ordinary thinking, feeling, willing and so on, because, first, this is the level which psychologists study. Although we have books on the psychology of religion, it seems to me that these are usually on psychological reactions to religion rather than on religion itself. By psychological reactions to religion I mean emotional states, desires, beliefs, built up by reasoning, habitual association, and so on, on the themes with which the genuine religion of spiritual values deals. Secondly, there is a very long and important tradition in philosophy, as well as mysticism, of using the words "psychology" or "psychologism" just for this limitation of view: one which cuts out the consideration of *values* and attempts to deal solely with the matter of emotions, feelings, senses, and so on, at the physical level. This is utterly wrong, not only from the mystical point of view but also from the point of view of philosophy, and that is why Descartes, Husserl and other philosophers have relentlessly attacked psychologism. The limitation to psychology in that sense is the complete enemy of philosophy as well as of mysticism.

The danger of it being, I suppose, that it is reductionist, and tends to reduce everything else to this level, and to regard the other levels of epistemology as non-existent, or else unnecessary.

Or else as a kind of epiphenomenon, something erected as an artificial structure on the basis of the physical and psychological.

This perhaps is what Collingwood was saying in his comments on William James, in his Autobiography: *that here psychology was attempting to do more than it could do, to make leaps that were totally unjustified.*

On the other hand I would have said that in his *Varieties* James does very subtly reach out from the psychological level towards the level of mystical values, which loom tremendously large further on in the book. He says, several times in effect, "We can't make sense of what's gone before without going on to the mystical level." Again, there is not a complete break between the psychological and the mystical, except in the sense that we have to control and detach ourselves from the psychological in order to reach the mystical. We have to use our physical-level powers all the time, but they must be under control from the mystical level; they must be guided by wisdom, obedience, detachment, and by a knowledge of the Source, or whatever you like to call it.

What you're saying is that you've got to start from above, that it's no good starting from below and thinking you'll move upwards?

That's right; all genuine control comes from above, that is to say, above the psychological level.

But we always have to start from below.

Knowledge starts from below, but not genuine control; also of course the kind of knowledge that starts from below is a limited knowledge, a knowledge of facts, whereas real knowledge is a knowledge of structure, and that must come from above.

How does it come from above?

Here again I think we need to realise the difference between reasoning, the discursive powers, on the one hand, and the intuitive powers, the powers that reach essentially outside or beyond time to universals, on the other hand. When using the discursive powers we work from presuppositions; theories guide us. That's no good, where insight into ultimates is concerned. For that we have to rise above discursive processes to a level where truth presents it as a wholeness, and the mind sees the whole and at the same time the rational connections, without resting on any theory. Until we reach that level, our lower-level conclusions are likely to be vitiated by obscurity or error from the word go. Only intuition can justify any reasoning, in so far as it can be justified.

How would you see the relationship between this mystical perception and the belief systems of theology?

Most theological systems have originated in the use of special forms of language by mystics in order to convey their insights. I think this is particularly true of the theology of St. Paul and St. John. The danger, of course, is that the special language forms which have been devised in the first place by mystics for communication then become ossified by people who don't have their background; and then fixations become prevalent. The language forms are fixed on: the insight is lost. For a time these language forms will be useful for many people and will have a very powerful effect, in some cases a completely determining effect, on their whole life-span. For other people, and for most people today, they may be useless and may even lead them seriously astray because the language forms are misinterpreted.

Do you think the materialistic preoccupation of our age has blinded us, so that our perception is clogged, or has this always been the case?

To some extent the world has always had different groups of people; some clogged, others open. The materialistic outlook, or rather the scientific outlook which came in about the seventeenth century, has worked in two ways. In one way it has produced a great objectivity, a great clarification, a great freeing from things like superstition; it has released people from too tight a dependence on doctrine. In another way it has filled their minds with wrong and constricting ideas which prevent them from searching out in intuitive ways; a system has been given them and it has in effect become another religious doctrine.

You mean it's a system that's closed and all-explanatory, so that they don't try to look for anything beyond it.

Yes. The scientific outlook tends to fall into the same fault as theology does; but it takes people in different ways. Some will lap up the teachings, become more closed in their outlook, and say, "Now this is a complete explanation; now I can rest, and go ahead with my practical work". Other people say, "I can't bear such a restricted outlook, there's something sham about it; I'm going to look deeper". And I think in science there has never been a time when some scientists haven't tried to look deeper, some of them very deep indeed.

And do you feel that the quantum and relativity revolution in physics during this century has given an extra impetus to this, by overthrowing the nice orderly pattern which physical science seemed to offer?

Yes, this is a point which I feel should be made very strongly. We must fill the world with the knowledge that the mechanistic outlook of the nineteenth century just won't work; it's wrong in principle. It has served its purpose, and is now doing immense harm. We must stress by all means possible that modern physics does not take that viewpoint.

How far do you think that the higher levels, and the self-evident certainties which are revealed by the logos, *can form a paradigm for the investigation of religious experience?*

After one has made an initial, external, so to speak "face-value" classification, I think that to make sense of the phenomena one has to approach from a higher, philosophical, mystical level; for the reason that considerations of structure, interconnection, value and so on are higher-level considerations. We shall only, therefore, put a true ordering on these things if we single out those parts which purport to come from a higher level. As I looked through some of your examples, I felt I could quite clearly see those parts of the experiences which came from a higher level and those which one might call subjective additions. Some of the examples refer to types of cognition or perception which are recognizably proper to God as transcendent, the highest level: there is, for instance, the tremendous, enveloping reality to which one turns, releasing one, opening out. The best of them use very expressive language: the intensity of the experience is such that suitable words come, and one can usually tell at once, if one has read many of these accounts, which are authentic and which are not. From the use of the metaphysical terms one can see where the experience shifted to a mystical level, or where the mystical character came through most strongly. To take an example: "I suddenly saw the world as if it had always been there; there was no gap, no barrier, all was inextricably bound, continuing, one great Being." This is definitely metaphysical, and I would say the metaphysical language here, "inextricably bound", "no barrier", "continuing, one great Being", at once puts it in the mystical category. Looking at the same account again, we might find some psychological additions, though it may be difficult to be sure of their character without further questioning of the person concerned. For instance, here: "Light, Life and Joy mingled with Pain, Darkness and Death, until the idea of a Transcendent Being no longer held." I find myself having to study this account of experience in great detail to realise its nature, and cannot be sure exactly what the experience was at each stage. But I think the more we read these accounts the easier it maybe to classify them from the higher level. Just before, the lady who wrote this account says, "I felt with wonderful anticipation that God was coming back to me." There it appears that she was not, at that stage of life, aware that there was any sort of transcendent reality. Theoretically she thought there must be; she had some memories of it, but the awareness wasn't there at the time. There are such theoretical awarenesses, like doctrines or theories; and so far as they are doctrines or theories, they are not mystical. Nevertheless they can help forward a mystical experience. So, as this precedes the passage about "Light, Life and Joy", I would say we should probably interpret the latter not in a mystical sense but in a psychological one, working towards the mystical. Thus I think "Light" here means, "Now I am getting somewhere"; but it's not the vision of transcendent, archetypal light. "Life" means a feeling that now things are becoming more real, and "Joy mingled with Pain" — this is more psychological again. At this stage the experience as a whole is largely psychological, but behind the scenes there is a groping forward towards a remembered mystical. Later she says, "Until the idea of a Transcendent Being no longer held"; here the groping part crushed out the memory of what God was like as transcendent. She goes on, "But God seemed personal, intimately concerned with the world and ever-present". There is a shift here, as if to the paradigm of immanence. (I distinguish these paradigms, God as transcendent, God as immanent; they are interlocked, of course, but one can be emphasized more than the other.) So after this period of apparently losing God as transcendent, God as immanent began to grow in her. She "saw things as an ever-flowing stream, with God as the source and the current". This is a bit mixed again: it's coming back to transcendence, with God as the Source.

But this mixture is surely characteristic of a great deal of such experience?

Yes, first one aspect comes through, then another, till they ultimately blend, or are seen to be perfectly compatible. So this experience seems to portray a kind of shuttling back and forth, from the age of fifteen onwards, from transcendence to immanence and back to transcendence. Lastly she says, "I had a breakthrough, an experience from which I felt there was no return". Now looking closely at this language I seized at once on the phrase "no return". This feature is characteristic of religious experience: the ultimacy of it. Once it happens as a rebirth, nothing can be the same after it. And one is conscious that there is a continuation. If the exaltation comes and goes, it can be largely psychological in character. So the words "no return" are a clue to me. On that ground alone I would say the writer has now reached the mystical level almost certainly. It was made perfectly clear by the words that followed. At this stage she is recounting a mystical experience; before it was a psychological one. Now she says: "I suddenly saw" — the revelation, if it is very powerful, comes abruptly but then eases away gradually — "I suddenly saw the world as if it had always been there." I was particularly thrilled by that! Before the world was, I AM. There's something of the eternal about it: "The first and the last, the Alpha and the Omega". It's a wonderful way of putting it, because it's not a stock way. It's not a quotation, it just came spontaneously. The truth has come through, and it has gone into words miraculously fitting — "the world as if it had always been there". Now we go on to words that are all mystical: "There was no gap, no barrier; all was inextricably bound, continuing, one great Being." Every one of these expressions has point mystically, but is nonsense physically. Fixation has disappeared; universality has taken over.

Is your recognition of the mystical quality of this due to a communion of feeling, and the fact that you yourself share an understanding of what she means, are part of the community of those who would talk the same language?

Partly that; but on the other hand, this is not my particular language. I would never use the words "inextricably bound" because "bound" suggests to me fixation. I wouldn't use it, but I can see what she means in the context. Perhaps it does strike home to me, because of my background, more than to an ordinary person. But at the same time I would have thought that on most people who had any idea of what was religious it would make a strong impact.

How would you account for the fact that quite a lot of people describe an experience like this, and then say, "I have never had anything as vivid as this since"; while others will say, "This has provided a sense of direction for my whole life"? There seems to be a time for some people when they are particularly open to this kind of experience, but it's an openness which some appear to lose.

There are various possibilities to explain why an early openness falls off, and one would have to ask for a person's life-history to decide between them. One of the ways it could fall off is through too whole-hearted an immersion in matters of discursive reasoning, or worldly administration. Such attitudes or occupations raise a big problem for the mystic, making the detachment which is needed for sustained awareness of the higher levels very difficult. The fall-off can then be so complete that one almost comes to the opinion that the higher levels don't exist. In the case of those who have never experienced the higher levels in their intensity, these lower entanglements fix them very strongly in the view that the higher levels can't possibly exist, and that it's nonsense to talk about them; to talk about another world just doesn't make sense to them. But if one has had a fully-fledged mystical experience, and is not going through a specially "dark" phase, I think the memory and openness are not lost, so talking about another world is just talking about matters of fact.

I wonder what you would say about an account written by a woman who describes an experience of rebirth while lying in bed — she had not been very well and was feeling depressed — and this sense of complete newness of life lasted for some weeks but then gradually faded away, and was replaced by a condition almost worse than her original one; so that she felt that the Spirit of God had deserted the world.

This is quite typical of what they call aridity. An experience of mystical renewal may last for some time, months, or days. Its renewing effect must last longer than a few minutes, otherwise I do not think it would be well called mystical. But sooner or later there will be a lapse of some kind.

But what is it that is missing there? Is it a lack of response, or a lack of obedience?

I would rather say that we have evidence here that the mystical teaching is in advance of the person's actual spiritual situation. The experience is like a teacher; it gives something a little too difficult, and then you have to grow into it. Every one of these mystical revelations has to root itself in you. You have to go through a time when it has to find its mature fulfilment, and this necessarily involves a certain kind of dark night or struggle, till it becomes your own. I would say that in every case the teaching that is given to one is in advance of one's real capacity; there's something in one that gives it root, but we can't really live in it fully as we haven't developed adequate powers of response; these have to develop afterwards.

When earlier on you spoke of self-discipline, it was presumably to do with remaining detached from administration and so on. What will help the administrator to remain detached in order to be open to the experience of the higher levels?

In the first place the administrator must be fully aware of the danger of getting too caught up in what is merely external, what is discursive rather than holistic. There must always be some sort of wrestling to detach oneself. It's difficult to generalize, because I believe that some kinds of activity, particularly creative activity (such as that of the artist), can be maintained without being cut off from the higher level. There's a particular outgoing power in what we call inspiration, for instance, when we are conscious of the two levels at once. We can't guarantee such a spontaneous doubly-conscious state; it may happen for a minute or in some degree for months. It is possible to have the two levels intimately fused, and then the power comes through tremendously. Even in ordinary circumstances one should realise that something of this kind is possible; and one must strive to keep onself sufficiently detached, watchful, uncaught up in fixation, while involved in administration, to feel that one hasn't lost oneself. Various mystical books stress that one of the important things before taking up any task is to collect oneself and, to put it rather crudely, offer up a prayer, align oneself to the Source, prepare oneself by orienting oneself for energy; and in a curious way, if one prepares oneself by an attitude of devotion, the power does come in and one doesn't forget one's alignment. Unless you go on for too long, of course. And all the time, if one is watching, one feels that the Source, the Power, the Wisdom is sufficiently with one to prevent one getting too involved. If one is watching sufficiently, and then finds oneself getting too caught up, one is instantly aware of the fixation, and again a kind of wrestling or prayer goes up and one detaches oneself. All the time this wrestling should be going on, in the background or powerfully present. So we have two chief possibilities: either the Power comes in sufficiently to fuse the two levels, and we have a state of inspiration, or it comes through with lesser power and we are conscious of a kind of wrestling, all the time reorienting ourselves to the Wisdom. I suppose that is what every one of us does when watchful and conscientious. All the time we are trying to behave wisely, we are trying to put aside sillinesses, and discomforts of mind where we feel we have lost a grip of ourselves. There isn't a complete cleavage between the two. But on the other hand one can get completely entangled in the lower level so as to lose sight of the higher, if one doesn't take the initial viewpoint that it's possible to wrestle in this way and keep some sort of alignment with the Source.

Would you say that fixation with the lower level is rather too predominant in our whole educational tradition? We are so caught up with "subjects", with passing this level and that, with sheer achievement and the acquisition of knowledge.

Certainly. In ordinary education there doesn't seem to be any acknowledgement of the need for an intuition of guiding wisdom. You just have to accept what is given to you outwardly, almost as a formula!

You hint at a technique of "wrestling". Could you say something more about it? for instance how often should the administrator "offer up a prayer"? Daily? Weekly?

The general attitude must be continuous. The danger is this: one may occasionally remind oneself, "I know the right and the good is there to guide me"; but the adherence is not sufficiently habitual. Suddenly there may be a distraction, or something goes wrong; I became conscious of the effects of entanglement, of fixation. What one must not do is to lose one's grip and say, in effect, "I can't concern myself with that now, but in five minutes' time I'll offer up a prayer". On the instant — this is the action of the Cross, on one who is continuously obedient in his heart — as soon as the least fixation occurs, the automatic response would be the uplift, the restoration of freedom and obedience. And this will happen if we are sufficiently continuous about watching.

Michael Polanyi, in his analysis of the inspiration of the scientist, saw two elements in genius: the immense effort, and also the moment of inspiration, which is completely spontaneous and involves no effort at all. And he says usually the two go together. Is what you're talking about related to this?

It connects up very closely with what I was saying. There is in fact quite a lot of background research on this. Helmholtz was, I think, the first to analyse scientific inspiration, and further work on this was done by various Frenchmen, including Poincaré; his scheme is the most famous. It connects up with the four mystical quarters, or "directions of spirit" as I call them. The stages in Poincaré's scheme are:
1. The *preparation*, in which you do your work in an energetic and determined but more or less mechanical way, collecting material without knowing quite where it's going to lead; this is the outgoing of the spirit, a sort of groping about at the lower level. Then you have:
2. The *incubation*. This is very important; all mysticism begins with "letting go". Then there is:
3. The spontaneous *illumination*, and:
4. The *working out* (Poincaré calls it the "precising"). Once the inspiration has come it has to be worked out so that you can make it your own. There has to be a clarification, a unification, a synthesis.

These four stages are related to the four mystical quarters, symbolized by the motion of the sun. The *preparation* is like the setting sun, because you relinquish your hold on the inner wisdom in order to grope about on the outskirts, so to speak; the sun is allowed to set in order for you to get new material. The danger is of altogether losing sight of the sun, which is the source of wisdom, and of falling into a kind of spiritual death. The proper attitude is to allow oneself to "go out", realizing that this must be followed or synthesized automatically by a *letting-go.* One must apply oneself and at the same time have non-attachment. Now we go on to the northern quarter, where the sun is actually out of sight; the divine light works in secret. And then the sun rises in the east and we have the flash of illumination, the new light coming in. Finally it rises to its height in the south and works itself out; everything grows and is fruitful.

Could I ask how far the particular conditions of your own youth led you to mystical experiences? You describe in your book how you came to feel that mental images were somehow more real than the things you perceived in the outside world; and then you describe a great self-consciousness about your body, and later how you became aware of having a proper spiritual form, quite different from your usual everyday body. Would you say there was a connection between your early shame of your body and these later experiences? Or is this asking a question which is psychological in a bad sense?

To begin with I don't think "shame" is the right word. It may not even have been the right word for Plotinus. What I felt had a cognitive quality; there was a kind of cognition that things were not right, that there was an ideal that I had to work for. Where that ideal came from I wouldn't like to say. You could perhaps trace it back in my life, or if you believe in reincarnation perhaps even further! Quite what began the conscious search for the mystical in my life is very difficult to say. I shouldn't say it was awareness of being in the wrong body, because I think something probably came before that. Frequently there was a curious experience of the walls of the room receding. This was an experience I had at the age of four or five, for a couple of years I should think. These were, I now think, preparatory experiences for getting into the spirit: the spatial barriers dissolving. This then led to the feeling that the body was not mine; the bodily identification had been dissolved as well as the walls of the room. From that point on, something had to be done; I had to devise or discover techniques. If one asks now about these techniques, I would say they come down in the first place to self-discipline; but one must look further and ask how the self-discipline is done, what is the essential principle. It is done by, in effect, stopping time; here the eternal is first revealed. If we don't have the ability to stop time, then we don't have spiritual control. We must face up to things which are unpleasant and stop time over them, and then the releasing power comes in automatically. If we have merely the consciousness that things are not right, then provided we face up to them and stop time over them, we become released. So what followed can be described as an endeavour to get released from everything in life — sight, hearing, feeling, and so on — by a practice of stopping time. This is the practice called "recollection". Eventually there comes an awareness of drawing oneself back to the Wisdom, the recollection of God; but in the early stages the practice is more like a recollecting of one's freedom.

Some people when meditating take something they can see and bear that in mind, and even if thoughts come and go they hold on to this. This has the effect of arresting the stream of consciousness. Do you think this is at all helpful?

It is possible to watch a material object continually while time still flows, one impression after another. That is not the practice of "recollection", though it might be of some use to correct a tendency to mind-wandering. But if one takes some "pure ideas" in the sensory impression at some one instant, say the particular shade of green at some point or the angle made by two lines, and dwells on this idea and instant so that one is not carried along by time, but feels unchangingness and release, then there would be successive acts of recollection. In that case it is generally better, I think, *not* to take always the same material object, but to let one's choice of detail to recollect be governed freely by the interest it evokes. People practise what they call "meditation" in so many ways that I find it impossible to generalise. If a meditation session merely results in a person shutting his eyes, vaguely trying to quieten the mind and hoping for something to happen, I don't think it gets anywhere. Another method is to repeat a word continually, as a magical device, to give the mind something to do and so prevent mind-wandering or tensions building up. Far better, I think, is to watch for signs of tension and use words such as "relax" to help create an open, unified state of watchful ease. But I am not even very happy about this if it is done only in certain sessions when one sits down, shuts one's eyes, and continues for the required ten minutes or so. This to my mind shuts off the free response to what is right and good, to the Wisdom as it arises in us: it's not a very obedient attitude, and certainly not continuous or habitual. And the prime requisite is that we should be habitually obedient; what we have to watch above all is the guiding light or voice telling us what is right and good, *each instant*. And then comes some kind of recollection practice, as prompted by that obedient watching. If the word "meditation" is to be restricted to some definitely profitable kind of practice, in accord with its etymology and common meaning as a frequentative word, I think it should be kept for practices which have the effect of replacing the discursive tendency by intuitive watching, even if this is not recollection. The process of checking tensions and mind-wandering by pulling oneself up, creating better freedom, and then trying to watch specific details of feeling or thought, may then spread to the whole of life, including sense-observation, with the eyes open. Then one is ready for the thoroughgoing practice of recollection. So, eventually, one finds a continuous state where effort is not needed. The open attitude becomes habitual; one becomes always in some degree conscious of obedience, of the world of spirit as a vehicle for guidance. But one must start with "bits and pieces" because it's the only way to start getting control.

You were implying earlier on that if someone claims knowledge of God, but no fixations are released, then the claim must be false.

If their view of higher things is blocked by fixation, then they couldn't speak understandingly of them; they couldn't know God.

But they might still claim to; their claim might be an aspect of their fixation, as in conventional religion.

There are many ways of knowing God, in the mystics' sense of the words, and there are many kinds of experience on which a claim to know God might be based. In conventional religion it seems to me doubtful whether many of the people who repeat the formulas or take part in the rites would actually claim to know God. Putting aside the various mystical knowledges of God, I suppose we are here concerned with people who have experienced some state of euphoria, or who have formed some code of beliefs and participate in practices which they consider to establish for them a higher communion. Experiences of these kinds might be described as preliminaries to the way, useful to some people and in some ages, but seldom touching the essentials of the way itself. One enters the mystical way on realising the difference between fixation and freedom, and the fact that by facing up to fixation in an open way, obedient to Wisdom, a divine power enters and takes us into a unitary release. This is the principle of divine incarnation, which is the great principle of spiritual progress.

And would you say that these same principles apply to all forms of human activity? What Polanyi is trying to show is that there is an unbroken transition from the activity of the scientist, with his preoccupation with "bare facts", right the way through to that of the poet; a continuous spectrum, with the same principles applying throughout. What you are saying seems to fit in with this.

Yes, it's most important to realise that this direct releasing process is fundamental to the whole of life. Of course one can see things more clearly at a higher level. At a lower level this might seem like a kind of hypothesis, a pleasant or helpful idea; but at the higher levels, and the further one goes through this releasing process, the more one begins to see clearly what is happening. For instance, if one sees a beautiful natural scene, one may vaguely feel that there is something deep and spiritual in it. But if one sees beauty at a higher level, it is the same thing as ultimate purity. In the natural scene this has somehow become fused, merged or blended with the physical. What is confused in natural beauty can be seen in its purity out of the body, or at any rate in a more pure form, so that one can sense the intelligible structure of things in a way not possible at the lower levels.

Could you tell us what, in your view, is the place of the demonic in all this, and how one first becomes aware of it?

One very important point that doesn't I think always appear, even from mystical descriptions, is that you can't see the demonic unless you are fortified by divine power. The demonic seen as demonic is a divine revelation of what is against spiritual goodness and wisdom. This revelation of the "againstness" of something is a tremendous good as a protection; it is the revelation of evil in its true, its proper nature. First of all in human life, we are immersed in those evils of fixation, wrong tendencies that drag us down or impede progress, and we take them to our hearts and say, in effect, "This is me, I've got a desire, I want to do this", and so on; we take these feelings to ourselves. The next stage is to feel that something is not right; we feel a bit ashamed, or a bit guilty; but we can't be objective about it. Perhaps the next stage is to become a little more detached and "sleep on it", and in course of time to get rid of the anguish. But there's still another stage, and that is of completely facing up to it, and aligning ourselves at the same time with the great saving and healing power; in this way we may be able to see the wrong tendency revealed in its true, ultimate nature. To see it revealed in its ultimate nature means that it must be represented in some way that is specially compelling and can contain the truth. It must be tremendously powerful; we must see the full dangers. For that we need to be divinely protected, as if by a steel casing between us and it; then it can be revealed. But when revealed in that way a wrong tendency is no longer evil for us. The revealing power is a tremendous good, and when those tendencies are revealed one can see how they are an integral part of creation. We have to go through this entanglement, this darkness. This is all part of the system. We can't begin straight away with maturity and total wisdom; we begin in darkness. Nevertheless certain things are terribly dangerous in that relatively unformed state. Certain things are helpful; other things can drag us down. And if we were to see clearly enough, then we should see that the things that drag us down are in divine order characterised in a certain way, even "placed" in a certain way. They are represented as below; they are represented as horrifying in certain ways, partly as a protective device, partly, because all these representations are — logically fitting, shall we say. And then conversely, up above in the higher worlds, when the distractions have been reduced to order and there is nothing but harmony, then the representations of life will be in correspondingly perfectly beautiful and fitting forms. Everything is absolutely just and according to logic; everything has its place. If we say demonic appearances are horrible and terrifying and take them to our hearts and fill ourselves with horror and terror, we are getting involved in fixation again. We had a little light which shows things as they are, and then we get involved in emotion again. But if we avoid that, if we look at the thing in a more completely detached way, we can say that the horror and fear are characteristics which we can view objectively. They are characteristics of the divine power, the divine dread, which are attached to these things on purpose, as a protective device to ensure that we can recognise them in their true nature.

I can understand that in terms of Christ.

Yes, the first and the last. And so if the archetype of humanity was from before the world began, in the inner structure of everything, then the animals represent stages towards the revelation of something which is more interior spiritually: and likewise with manifestations of the demonic. They take such forms only because representations have to be developed; and everything has a course of development from what is imperfect.

You spoke just now of everything being "absolutely just and according to logic". Could you say a little more about how you see this logic, this logos, *and how it is related to the discursive reason that we much need to counter?*

I make a distinction between reason and reasoning. Reasoning means for me what is discursive, step to step, depending upon some theory, axioms or presuppositions. This is not mystical; it will not open us to anything spiritual. One should be able to rise above the discursive attitude, as it were, on a kind of mountain-peak above it, so that you can look on discursive arguments, if you want to, and use them for teaching purposes at the lower level.

It's odd how few people have been concerned to pursue this very fundamental truth; and those that have, have been ignored, or have not been popular. How do you account for this seemingly voluntary blindness to something so important?

I suppose it goes absolutely against all ordinary scientific traditions. The hypothetico-deductive method which is supposed to be the kernel of science is based on step by step argument. One is brought up with the idea, if one is a scientist, that the only way to proceed intelligently is to make hypotheses and then work from them. It isn't the way of mathematics, though. Mathematics, I always say, is an art of intuition. In fact when I was studying for my Ph.D. in Maths, I was told by my supervisor not to worry about proofs; for one can concoct a proof any time one wants to, provided one sees what the truth is. The great thing is to get an idea of what the truth is first, intuitively, then you concoct your proof afterwards. Very often there can be three or four proofs on quite different lines. The essential thing is the insight. So in mathematics one gets a corrective to the traditional philosophy of science. Of course the experimental method must proceed from hypotheses; it must use deductive processes. One is too much in the dark to understand much of nature directly, so heuristic methods are needed.

The experiment is designed always to test some particular hypothesis.

Without the hypothesis you would have no starting point for experimentation. It's only at a later stage when one has done a variety of experimental work that one stands away and tries to synthesize it, to see the connections intuitively as a whole.

How far would you say that religious experience and mystical experience are the same? Or how far do they overlap? Which represents the larger area?

To me "religion" suggests a much wider area than "mysticism". One must accept a certain conventional use of the term "religious". For example when we talk of a religious service we are using the term "religious" in a sort of social sense. But such an experience, I mean of a religious service, couldn't normally be called mystical. I only use the term "mystical" if there is a clear indication that there is recognition — a cognition, a response to what one could call a centre or a source of something which is ultimate. Now in a religious service I would say that one could not expect from anyone present that degree of acknowledged cognition of the ultimate that I would call mystical. I have been giving some thought as to whether I could possibly make any suggestion as to how one might reduce these cases of yours to a more primitive order. It seemed to me that the first thing to do, if I were asked for advice over this, was to institute three fundamental categories. We have to start with some sort of initial classification. This involves, first of all, definitely clarifying our usage of the terms "religious" and "mystical". This is a rather conventional stage; we make up our minds how the word "religion" is to be used. In the same way, we have to decide what shall be called "intermediate" or "psychical". Such things as precognition I wouldn't generally call mystical; but I wouldn't call them physical either; they come in between. We must find, therefore, a form of words which is useful in an exploratory way to separate these three categories.

Are you then to some extent identifying the mystical and the religious?

I consider the mystical to be paradigmatic in character: in other words, so clear-cut that you can say definitely, this is one well-defined type of mystical experience, this is another type, and so on. In every case there must be definite recognition of an *ultimate* Wisdom and Reality, to be called "God", as Source (transcendent or immanent), and this implies also some definite awareness of transformation and unitary release. What is "mystical" is to be called "religious", but what is "religious" may not be "mystical". In the latter case there will only be a general sense of orientation to higher values, or if there is also a sense of divine Presence this will be overlaid and confused by psychological reactions — overbeliefs, shifting emotional states, extraneous thoughts, desires — so that the clear-cut unitary character is lost. One would have to give examples showing what the difference is, and it would naturally be very difficult to specify where the line comes, in terms satisfying to a scientist.

We have had the same difficulty. We began by thinking in terms of two main divisions: the mystical and the religious. The latter includes those feelings that people may have of being in touch with some transcendental power beyond the self, without having the more dramatic or ecstatic kind of mystical experience. But when we came to examine them so many cases seemed to fall into both categories. A person may have some particular experience of a mystical kind, and this may lead him to take a quite different view of the world and so to become religious in a way he was not before. You however do not really make a sharp distinction between the mystical and the religious.

Well, I have proposed to take the religious as including the mystical, the mystical being so to speak a specialized, concentrated and pure form of it. Then come the intermediate, the psychical, and at ground level the physical and the psychological.

Could you elucidate a little the distinction you draw between these two lower stages, the psychical and the psychological?

Precognition I think brings out the distinction very strikingly. The breach with the laws of time, the physical laws, is so complete, that one couldn't possibly call it a *physical* experience. Moreover it comes in an altered state of consciousness so that we have to say that a boundary has been stepped over. At the same time I would not describe precognition as psychological, or at any rate *normally* psychological. By the "psychological" I understand a kind of mental activity which lacks mystically or psychically objective cognition. Thus I don't much like Schleiermacher's emphasis on the *feeling* of dependence as characteristic of religious experience; it suggests too much of a psychological attitude. I think that throughout mysticism one must emphasize that it's cognitive: one *knows* something. And this is not merely cognition of a relationship or a truth, as that 2 + 3 = 5. It's cognition of something which is *real,* some *power* which exists. If this element comes through in any way, then the experience is religious, as against being psychological.

This is the element that William James called the "noetic", isn't it?

Yes, the experience must have a noetic quality. And then of course there is our own response. If there is cognition of ultra-physical reality and power then we must respond in the right way. This would either be by an attitude of love and obedience, or by awe and similar attitudes, leaving the door open for a response to the divine dread, the lower aspects of the divine power, which I think must be allowed to come into the religious as well as the mystical.

Well, that is my attempt to produce some indication as to what at the moment I would like to see the word "religious" mean, in a strict sense.

The intermediate states would then be distinguished by the fact that there is not in them that cognition of an ultimate reality and power. In precognition, for instance, I don't think one usually has such cognition. One has cognition all right, but the element of the ultimate doesn't come through. The mind is not open in that way, so the experience doesn't have religious quality. But if the precognition is linked to, or is a vehicle of, the cognition of ultimate power or reality, then it would at once become religious experience.

One of the problems to me is this: it seems that two people may have similar experiences, say of a psychic nature; and to one of them his experience may be of religious significance, while to the other his is not. It appears that it is the response which a person, consciously or unconsciously, is able to make to an experience that decides whether that experience is to be regarded as religious or not.

Wouldn't you say, though, that the response is determined by something in the experience itself, or is even part of it? If one says that the difference between a religious experience and one that is not religious lies merely in the response, then one is making that difference merely subjective.

Yes, but perhaps this is right. Doesn't one of the difficulties lie in the difference of people's presuppositions? One meets some people for whom every experience of a particular kind is an encounter with God, is a religious experience, because by upbringing or conditioning they are predisposed to this way of thinking; whereas another person in similar circumstances would be naturally more sceptical. So it must always be open to question whether an intuition of reality is pure, or is just the result of assuming that it's God. One knows oneself that one can react differently at different times to the same kind of experience.

First of all one must take each experience not as a "kind" but exactly as it is in its entirety, and contemplate it as an observer, as a scientist; and then one must try to read the account very carefully, or question the person concerned very carefully, to discover how much is a genuine report of what happened on that occasion and how much is due to an overbelief or something read into it, for which the experience itself gives no warrant. There may be some accounts which are completely bogus, so to speak, in the sense that what is described may have been merely a moving emotional experience into which religious ideas have been read and forced, and the terminology of other experiences has been taken over without proper warrant in the experience itself. It doesn't often happen but I think it sometimes does. Nevertheless I think one can tell if one looks very carefully what are overbeliefs, what are presuppositions, and what is genuine. There was that example I quoted earlier on: the person who described having had "a breakthrough, an experience from which I felt there was no return". The language used to describe that experience has just come spontaneously: the truth has come through, objectively, and it has gone into words miraculously fitting. It's perfectly open and sincere, not a matter of overbeliefs from extraneous sources.

But overbeliefs tend to merge with the experience, and to give it the form that it takes. One can distinguish between "response within an experience" and "response to an experience". It is actually within the experience itself that one's over-beliefs or inner convictions or whatever one likes to call them have their influence; they mould the form of the experience, and give it the significance that it has for one. Can one in these circumstances distinguish between stimulus and response?

I don't think one can, except when it is a matter of ultimates, that is to say mystical objectivity. Suppose you have the response of obedience; divine light is revealed, and one's whole being goes out to it, responding to the Right and the Good. Now can you separate the response from the Source, from the divine Right and Good which you obey? Surely you can. You must obey something; the whole rationale of the obedience is that there's a Source to obey, a great Wisdom to obey. So the distinction is in that case valid, and essential to the experience.

The overbelief here is not a sort of afterthought; it comes actually in the experience itself.

But I wouldn't call the obedience there an overbelief at all. What would be an overbelief would be if you said, "I obey like this because I'm a Christian".

You mean it would involve conscious reflection?

Yes, and reasoning too; going back to something else in time and forging a connection, or bringing in a presupposition.

If a person were to say that a certain moment the Holy Spirit had led him, would that involve an overbelief?

Normally yes, because the words "Holy Spirit" would probably have associations with the doctrine of the Trinity. They might not, of course; the man might have deliberately adopted the words "Holy Spirit" for that sort of experience.

You spoke just now of making the difference between a religious and a non-religious experience "subjective", an idea which you rejected. Perhaps I'm not quite so averse to the word as you are. There do seem to be certain types of experience that to one person may be profoundly significant, while to another they are not. The second person just does not respond to them in the same way as the first does.

Well, I wouldn't say they were the same type of experience. Take for example the experience of light. This may be mystical, it may be psychical, it may be psychological. If it is mystical, you will get in addition to the word light certain reports of universality, of ultimacy, of reality, of truth coming through automatically, because they are indissolubly involved in the mystical cognition of light. Light is the universal content of seeing. It's so intimately related to truth that you can't separate them in actuality at the higher levels. Now if the person says, "I saw a great light that remained whether my eyes were open or shut, but presently it disappeared," the whole tone of the experience sounds to me psychical; there's not a reference to anything ultimate at all. The fact that it was suddenly cut off suggests to me that it had no after-effects, it created no re-birth, no transformation was involved in it; it was just an experience that came and went. That would not, to me, be mystical. And yet the same term "light" would have been used. Now the difference between these two cases would not to my mind lie in the difference of the response in each case. I would say the responses were different because the experiences in their essence were different. You could of course argue that if the person's response had been different he would have been open to a different sort of experience; the two are naturally causally involved. But the fundamental category of difference here is between the mystical and the psychical, and the response is, so to speak, logically posterior.

There are people who describe experiences of being surrounded by a sort of golden light. They often say at the time they had a great feeling of exaltation, of great joy or ecstasy in relation to the light. One feels at once that such experiences are mystical.

Yes, these are strong indications that the light which they describe should be thought of as mystical. There's another experience described in your collection which I eventually decided I would call mystical, so far as the experience of light is concerned. It begins: "On the first night I knelt to say my prayers, of which I had now made a constant practice. I was aware of a glowing light." Now if it stopped there I would say we cannot be sure what kind of experience it is. It could be psychological, it could be psychical, it could be mystical. But then the description goes on . . . "which seemed to envelop me, and which was accompanied by a sense of warmth all round me". On the basis of these words, "which seemed to envelop me", I would classify the experience as mystical. To me, the phrase "a light enveloping" points beyond the physical level. "A light enveloping me" doesn't make sense physically. It seems to me here there's a definite attempt to convey the dissolution of boundaries and the universality which is characteristic of divine light. The experience being of the ultimately real and universal, the boundaries must fall; universality comes in. The mention of the word "enveloping" seems to me inexplicable unless there were something of this mystical content. But of course there could have been many psychological reactions too. As far as the sense of warmth goes, this could be mystical; as the enveloping light was almost certainly mystical, the warmth was probably mystical too. On the other hand it could have been almost physiological; one can get also a psychical feeling of warmth or cold, as for instance in seances where people feel cold. But I would be inclined to say that if the one was mystical, the other, the warmth, was mystical too, especially as the "sense of warmth all round me" again seems to lay emphasis on the universality.

Then there's the problem of what has been called "Nature Mysticism". This it seems to me can belong to any of several levels. If one looks at experiences of the great beauty of nature where the feelings are so strong that a man senses a power and a presence, and the boundaries fall so to speak, and he seems himself to be part of the scene — then I would say the universality of things is coming through; the experience has taken on a mystical and religious character. In fact one often reads of the world being interfused with a presence and so on; that sort of language is clearly religious. On the other hand if the account says merely that the world appeared extraordinarily beautiful, or that he walked around hardly realizing where he was, then I think one has to have second thoughts about it. "Walking about hardly realizing where he was" gives of course an indication that he had partly left this world. One is partly separated, one has partly come into the universal. But on the other hand I wouldn't say that that sort of language was quite strong enough, quite detailed enough, to satisfy me that the experience was mystical. I would put such experiences of great natural beauty normally into the intermediate level, and only exceptionally into the mystical level.

Do you think there's a parallel between what Otto calls the sense of the numinous and "nature mysticism"?

If, in responding to the beauty of nature, one is conscious of a kind of divinity in it, of a universal presence of power uplifting one, with a quality of ultimacy in it, or of a sense of being centred in some way, or of something drawing one's will, then I would call the experience religious. There is something numinous in it. But there are obviously occasions when people admire the beauty of nature and there is nothing religious involved; the line is difficult to draw. Some of the cases I have read which are described as cases of nature mysticism I would not call mystical. Others, where the author rejects the idea that the experience is religious, I would regard as religious because I seem to detect in them some acknowledgement of a higher power. I think one has to read the account very carefully and try to read between the lines and see if there is sufficient recognition of the ultimate, of the universal power, or boundaries being dissolved, before one can be confident that the experience is suitably called mystical and therefore also religious.

There isn't much that is cognitive in Otto's sense of the numinous is there? I imagine there could be, but the cognitive isn't an essential feature of it.

I think this is a weakness of his book: he passes too much over the cognitive aspects of mysticism. For instance he says that mysticism overstresses the non-rational, which to me is very wrong. The LOGOS is the fount of all rationality; the LOGOS you might say is the container of the divine power at work. So I would say the mystical is not in itself non-rational: it's the fount of rationality. But the trouble is it's so involved, so abstruse, so transcendent, that at the first glimpse of it it seems to be too difficult to grasp by our feeble powers of reason.

Some people are inclined to ask what purpose a mystical experience serves. Is it, they would say, more than a purely private experience?

One might as well ask what is the purpose of education. But to understand the function of mystical experience in life it may be helpful to consider the distinction drawn by St. Paul between Law and Grace. In principle no-one, whether as a mystic or not, should adopt the attitude: "I do this because the Law says so and so, or because it's moral to do so". This is theorized, it's argued for, it's presupposition. The result may be quite good; it may have rescued you under the circumstances. But in principle the proper attitude to take is to surrender ourself to the Right and the Good first, and the Right and the Good will tell you what you have to do. Obedience is not a subjection of yourself to a private world; it's the subjection of the will to whatever it is right to do, and you won't be able to do right and good in the world unless you have previously learnt to subject your will to the Right and the Good. It's an outgoing as well as an ingoing; at least that is how I use the word "obedience". During the revelation itself it appears to be purely an ingoing, because one is completely taken up by the reality; but the point is that this going in is quite inseparable from a going out; the process of creation involves an outgoing as well as an ingoing. So, at the instant the level falls, one feels the creative power coming in to express itself. How it expresses itself, there again you have to watch, and follow a sort of outer obedience. The light is not so clear, but it's strong enough to keep it in your background so to speak; you know whether you are being directed or not. But the distinction between the inner direction of the Right and the Good and self-seeking can only be made in the light of the higher obedience. And certainly the application of obedience should be universal, and not limited to what is "private".

Is the acknowledgement of the Right and the Good an intuitive process?

The Right and the Good in its essence is the first mystical archetype or paradigm that I mentioned: the knowledge of God as transcendent.

Then the transcendent is defined as equalling the Right and the Good?

It's inseparable in the Godhead. What is transcendent and ultimate is the Right and the Good.

So these are not moral terms?

They *are* moral, because the rightness or goodness of motives and actions is inseparable from the obedience which characterises the mystical way, and the mystical way is inseparable from the ultimate.

Many people would see the moral as something quite distinct from the mystical. There are many people whom we should call religious — they would consider themselves religious too — but yet would describe themselves as quite unmystical. Religion for them takes the form of an absolute imperative. Would you say such people were not religious?

I would say that an absolute imperative, being absolute, has meaning only in the context of the mystical way. Those who apprehend it vaguely and not mystically are then to be described as to that extent religious, especially if other things, too, show their orientation to ultimates. For such reasons I might even say that any awareness of conscience is religious.

Or perhaps a step on the way to *a religious experience?*

Yes, the working of conscience is an essential element in religious awareness, except that it is not very clear and is easily covered up by humanistic or doctrinal beliefs or emotional states. But at its root the working of conscience is the working of the Right and the Good in us.

There are many humanists who would deny any transcendence, and yet are very ethical. They have quite passionate feelings about the future of mankind, but deny that these feelings have any ultimate religious connotation.

I always wonder how far one can accept people's protestations when they say they don't believe in God or are not religious. It appears to me that in so far as a person behaves rightly and with an idea of goodness, he is actually aware of what I would call God; in that case, if he says he doesn't believe in God or in transcendence, I would say he has got the wrong conception of what I mean by the transcendent. In a sense, the Right and the Good *is* transcendent, because it's nothing you can point to in the physical world. I think very often people's theories run counter to their actual insights.

This is really a matter of terminology, then. Intellectually, people may claim to think in terms of one framework, while in fact they are revealing an acceptance of something rather different, which is much more metaphysical than they'll admit to?

Yes; it's like scientists who work with quantum theory or with relativity, and try to make out that their work is not ultimately based on metaphysics. They regard metaphysics as a dirty word. In the same way, to talk about the Right and the Good is metaphysical through and through. That agrees with the point I was trying to make before, that in the context of the mystical way everything becomes mystical (or at least religious), so long as you recognise that it *is* the mystical way; because then one recognises a higher orientation. Now this is the point where I think one has to make up one's mind that one's use of the world "religious" is to be fixed conventionally in a certain way. Are we going to admit that it is correctly used of the mystical way as a whole, provided there is a certain degree of awareness that it is the mystical way? The difficulty then is to say what sort of awareness we shall insist on, and how we are to detect it in any particular account. This is why I suggested defining the term "religious" in a strict sense, as applying to some definite here-and-now cognition of orientation to ultimates, even if it is a vague and general one. One should then perhaps admit also looser uses of the terms "religious" and "religion".

Some of these might be regarded as rudimentary?

Not only rudimentary. For instance, one may have a very clear awareness of the mystical way; one may adopt the ordinary practices of recollection, and they will take on a mystical quality because they are done from obedience. If they are done from self, however, and not from obedience, the experience would not be mystical or even strictly religious; but it might in some circumstances be described as loosely religious, for instance if the social context was religious in the broad sense. It's very difficult for one person to sense what degree of obedience another person is showing. That is why I think it would be difficult to decide that one account of some practice, such as ascetism, has a religious quality while another hasn't. My personal feeling is that once one knows where one is going, so to speak, and is watching the whole time, everything takes a religious character. But one's definition of "religious" becomes rather futile if everything can be religious.

But isn't that a rather fertile idea? Doesn't everything become religious for a religious man?

Notes on the participants

PETER BAELZ is Regius Professor of Moral and Pastoral Theology at Oxford and a Canon of Christ Church. His most recent book is entitled *The Forgotten Dream.*

CARMEN BLACKER became interested in Japan for no particular reason while still a child, and is now a lecturer in Japanese at Cambridge University. Her main interest is in Japanese Buddhism and folk religion, and her latest book is *The Catalpa Bow,* a study of Shamanistic practices in Japan.

CHRISTOPHER BRYANT is an Anglican Priest and a member of the Society of St. John the Evangelist (the Cowley Fathers). For many years he has been interested in Jungian psychology, and he is the author of *Depth Psychology and Religious Belief* and *The River Within* (to be published in 1978), both of which are concerned with the light shed by depth psychology on religion.

MONICA FURLONG is a writer and journalist and is now working with the BBC. Among her books have been *Journeying In* and *Contemplation Now.*

Archimandrite LEV GILLET is a priest of the Orthodox Church and Chaplain to the Fellowship of St. Alban and St. Sergius. He is the author of many books, including *Communion in the Messiah* (a study of Jewish-Christian relations) and *In His Presence.*

ROSALIND HEYWOOD is a Vice-president of the Society for Psychical Research; she is the author of *The Sixth Sense,* a historical sketch of research into ESP, and *The Infinite Hive,* a record of her own ESP-type experience.

MARTIN ISRAEL is an Anglican priest and Chairman of the Churches' Fellowship for Psychical and Spiritual Studies. He is also a Senior Lecturer in Pathology in the University of London. Among the books he has written are *Summons to Life* and *Precarious Living,* both of which are concerned with spiritual and psychical experience.

RAYNOR JOHNSON was lecturer in Physics in Queen's University,

Belfast and at King's College in the University of London, and from 1934 to 1964 was Master of Queen's College in the University of Melbourne. He is the author of a number of books, including *The Imprisoned Splendour, The Spiritual Path* and *A Pool of Reflections.*

Archimandrite KALLISTOS WARE is a priest of the Greek Orthodox Church and also Spalding Lecturer in Eastern Orthodox Studies at Oxford. He is the author of *The Orthodox Church* and editor of *The Art of Prayer: an Orthodox Anthology.*

MICHAEL WHITEMAN is Associate Professor Emeritus of Applied Mathematics at the University of Cape Town, and has contributed to a number of periodicals and symposia on psychology, para-psychology, physics and comparative religion. He is also the author of two books, *The Mystical Life* and *Philosophy of Space and Time.*

FREDA WINT was brought up in India and so assimilated many ideas from Indian culture. Later in England she turned away from Christianity and was attracted to the combination of the logical and the transcendent that she found in Buddhism. She studied Theravada Buddhism, and particularly meditation, in a monastery in north Thailand.